BURLAP & BUTTERFLIES

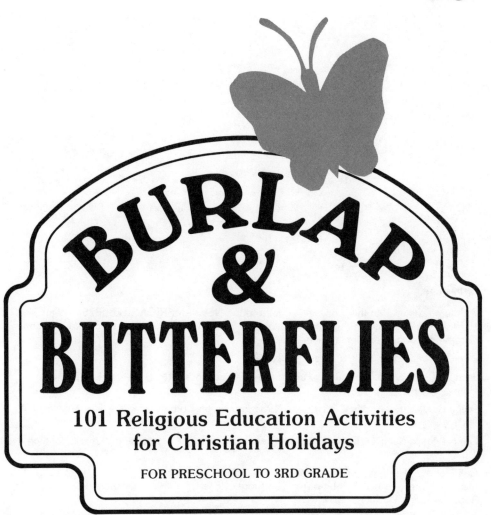

BURLAP & BUTTERFLIES

101 Religious Education Activities for Christian Holidays

FOR PRESCHOOL TO 3RD GRADE

• Patricia Mathson •

AVE MARIA PRESS
Notre Dame, Indiana 46556

Permissions

Scripture texts used in this work are taken from the NEW AMERICAN BIBLE, copyright © 1970, by the Confraternity of Christian Doctrine, Washington, D.C., are used by permission of copyright owner. All rights reserved.

Patricia L. Mathson, "Prayer Ideas," *Catechist*.

Jeanne Coolahan Mueller, *God's People Pray* (Minneapolis, MN: Augsburg Publishing House, 1984).

Peggy Bradley, *Family Meal Prayers* (© 1985 Franciscan Communications, Los Angeles, CA 90015).

Frances Kipps Spencer, *Chrismons Basic Series* (Danville, VA: Ascension Lutheran Church, 1972).

Gail Moody, "The Story of Pentecost"; Sue Ruddock, "Church Family Night"; Joan Lilja, "Jesus Is Born"; Patricia L. Mathson, "The Story of Easter"; *Church Teachers*, 2405 North Roxboro Street, Durham, NC 27704.

Gwen Costello, "Pentecost Play for Children"; Sister Delores McGinley, "Letters to God"; *Religion Teachers Journal*.

Helen Kitchell Evans, "Let Bells Ring," *Rainbows, Dreams, and Butterfly Wings*.

Library of Congress Catalog Card Number: 87-70841

International Standard Book Number: 0-87793-359-6

Cover design and illustrations: Elizabeth J. French

Printed and bound in the United States of America.

This book is dedicated
to my husband, Dick,
who has enriched my life
in so many ways.

Contents

Introduction

Life is a journey of growing in faith and along this path holidays are peak experiences for many children. If adults think back, they will likely remember holiday traditions that were important to them as children, and still are. Holiday memories last a lifetime.

Holidays remind us of God's presence in our lives. They offer opportunities for reflection and renewal. They remind us to make God the center of our lives and the focus of our Christian faith journey. Holiday activities and experiences help children explore their relationship with God.

Through Christian holidays we celebrate God's love for us, what he has done for us, and his continuing presence in our lives. Holidays remind us to praise God for his goodness and to express the joy we feel at being people of God.

By celebrating Christian holidays we witness to the presence of God in the world. We show others what we believe. We openly profess our beliefs and proclaim God's word to others whose lives we touch.

There are many ways to help children explore and celebrate Christian holidays. We need to provide activities that help children see the meaning of the Christian holidays for their own lives. Learning activities help us lead children to God by starting where they are in their lives and helping them grow in faith and the love of God.

Providing Variety in Religious Education Activities

Prayer is essential to Christian life and an important part of every holiday season. It helps children express their thoughts and feelings in dialogue with God. Learning different prayer forms helps children pray to God in all that they do and recognize that God is the center of their lives. Activities such as prayer links, class prayers, acrostics, songs, psalm prayers, action rhymes, petition prayers, blessing books and praise litanies help children express their feelings to God and praise him for his presence in their lives.

The *Bible* helps children recognize the presence of God in Christian holidays. The Bible is part of our Christian heritage. It tells the history of God and his people. It helps us understand our journey with God and find our place in the story of his people. Through the Bible God continues to reveal himself to us. The New Testament, which records what Jesus said and did, especially shapes our identity as Christians; we are expected to live the values of the gospels. Scripture helps us know and love God. Echo pantomimes, scripture chains, verse cards, stories, plays, puzzles, panoramas and spirals help children understand the message of Christian holidays through the Bible.

Art has been a universal way for people to express themselves, their ideas and their feelings. Art projects provide the opportunity for the hands-on learning that is so important for children. Take-home art projects remind children of the meaning of the holiday season. It is important to use a variety of art activities. Children like to explore creative ways of expressing themselves. Art projects help bring our sense of joy at being people of God into the classroom. Art helps children celebrate God's presence in their lives. Paper crafts, mosaics, drawings, cards, sticker art, ornaments, decorations, signs, posters and other art projects can be used successfully with children at holiday times.

Writing activities provide opportunities for children to think about what they are learning and to express it in their own words. Writing projects allow children time to reflect and focus their thoughts on the meaning of the holidays in their own lives. Essays, newsletters, poetry, letters, rhymes and notes help children express their ideas.

Review games are geared to the way children learn. Children like games because they add variety to the lesson and provide a challenge. Games are an excellent way to help children review words, ideas and concepts associated with the holidays. Games motivate children and hold their interest. Games also allow for self-directed learning. Question games, board games, matching games, symbol games, word games and other review games are excellent for use in religious education.

Group projects are essential in Christian education. Children need to learn to work together as a people of God. Community is what church is all about. Children have to experience and learn to be part of the faith community. It is within a community that we are called to minister to one another. By providing projects that involve the whole group, we show children what can be accomplished when people work toward a common goal. Group projects such as murals, leaf trees, round robins, altar cloths, pageants and banners stress community and help children celebrate holidays together.

Outreach projects help children learn to share the gift of God's love with others. They remind us that Christians care about others in the name of Jesus Christ. A caring attitude is not automatic but must be developed, nurtured and practiced. Outreach projects are reminders that we are to share our joy and our bounty with others in God's family. Hopefully the care and love that we show to others during holidays will carry over into our day-to-day lives. These projects take learning beyond the classroom and into the lives of the children. Food collections, sponsoring a child, angel trees, gifts, nursing home visits, placemats and rice bowl activities provide children with the opportunity to serve others in Jesus' name.

Using a variety of activities enhances understanding and reaches children with varied learning styles. The religious education classroom should be a place where children have the opportunity to explore new ideas and new ways of doing things under the guidance of the teacher. The children should be free to discover and explore the many facets of their relationship with God.

In the Classroom

God calls us all to life with him. It is for this that we were created. We must carefully nurture the faith of the children entrusted to us. Faith is a personal, ongoing relationship with God. It is a gift freely given to us by God. It is our privilege to help the children come to know and love God in their lives.

Teachers must provide an environment where learning can take place. The religious education classroom must be a place where all children are accepted and valued, where ideas and feelings can be freely shared. As witnesses to God's love, we should be communicating a message of love, caring and concern. Using positive expressions and words with the children encourages their cooperation by showing respect for their feelings and ideas. Actions as well as words help children learn that God loves them and cares about them.

Organization is important in activity-centered learning. Activities with children must be carefully planned. Everything should be set up before they arrive in the classroom. When activities are organized, class time flows more smoothly, the children are more involved, and both teacher and students find learning the enjoyable experience it should be.

Evaluation is also important. It helps us re-examine our goals and our methods. We need to make written notes about what works and what doesn't, about what should be done differently next time, and about activities that worked especially well. We must decide if enough activities are being planned to keep the children's attention and interest. Perhaps, on the other hand, too many activities are being crammed into too little time. This is common at holiday time. We must allow time for reflection and for learning to take place.

Hopefully this book will lead to other ideas and other activities. Each teacher must adapt the activities presented to his or her learning situation. Each age group is different, each class is different, each teacher is different. Activities must be selected, organized and presented so that they are meaningful to the group with whom they are used. The teacher must help God's love come alive for the children in concrete ways they can understand.

As teachers, we must above all have faith in God for whom we teach and remember that it is his message that we are called to proclaim. We must be people of faith ourselves before we can share that gift with others. We must always ask for God's help in teaching his children.

The following chapters present learning activities for the religious education of children. These activities are designed to supplement any Christian curriculum. They can be used in weekly religious education classes, Sunday school classes, parochial and church schools, parish celebrations, after-school programs, day care, preschool programs, family programs, intergenerational events — anywhere that children gather to learn about God and his presence in our holiday celebrations.

·1·

The Tradition of
THANKSGIVING

All that we are and all that we have are gifts from God. Our families, our friends, the warmth of the sun and the very food that we eat are gifts God gave us out of his unending love for us. The pilgrims understood this and gathered together with the local Indians to give thanks to God for a bountiful harvest.

This tradition of giving thanks has continued to this day. Each November we celebrate Thanksgiving. The very name of this holiday sums up what it is all about—a giving of thanks to our Creator. For some, this meaning may be overshadowed by plans for a big turkey dinner, but for all of us as God's people it should be a time when we pause to remember our many blessings.

Some families have developed longstanding Thanksgiving traditions centering on the whole family being together. Many churches have special Masses on Thanksgiving morning when people may bring their bread and wine and have it blessed for their holiday meal. In our classrooms we stress to the children that this is a time for joyful reflection on the many blessings in our lives, for prayers of thanksgiving, and for sharing with people who are less fortunate. In this way we help them see that Thanksgiving is a time of giving thanks to God.

Acrostic

In an acrostic prayer the first letter of each word begins with a letter in the theme word. For a prayer at Thanksgiving time the theme word, of course, is Thanksgiving.[1]

In order to write their own prayers, children must stop and think of some things for which they are thankful. An individual acrostic makes their prayer personal. A Thanksgiving acrostic turns out like the following one:

T rees

H ands

A nimals

N oses

K angaroos

S unshine

G iraffes

I ce cream

V acation

I nsects

N ighttime

G ames

The acrostic works well as a prayer form for children. It helps them order their thoughts. It provides a starting place for children who are just beginning to write their own prayers. It is a means of helping children express themselves to God through prayer.

Thanksgiving Tree

A Thanksgiving tree helps children realize that they have many, many things for which they can be thankful. The Thanksgiving tree is a good follow-up to a class discussion of the tradition and meaning behind the Thanksgiving holiday.

Before class, cut a tree shape out of green poster board. Make a large, round scalloped shape for the top. The trunk should be covered with wood-grain pattern self-adhesive covering. Put the tree on the class bulletin board and label it *Our Thanksgiving Tree*.

Ask the children to make leaves for the tree using the fall colors. In a large class each child can make one leaf. In a small class each child can make a leaf of each color. On each leaf the children print *Thank you, God, for* (the name of something for which they are thankful). This may be anything from friends to bikes to pets to sunsets to chocolate cake. As the children finish, let them glue their leaves on the tree. If the tree becomes crowded glue some leaves as if they are falling from the tree to the ground.

This makes a colorful bulletin board and also reminds children of blessings which they might not have thought of before. The profusion of leaves on the tree reminds them of the many, many blessings that we have from God.

The Thanksgiving tree helps children to put giving thanks back into Thanksgiving.

Action Rhyme

Action rhymes are short poems with simple gestures. They are an excellent way to help young children learn. Action rhymes capture the interest of the children. They involve the children in the lesson, and they are easy to remember.

Action rhymes are meaningful to children because they contain the essence of the lesson. The children have the opportunity to participate individually by saying the rhyme and doing the gestures. At the same time they are part of a group experience.

The following action rhyme is a wonderful one for the Thanksgiving season.[2]

We Thank You

We thank you, God, for sunshine bright,
(*Arms up, fingers touching to make sun.*)

For birds that sing at morning light,
(*Arms outstretched like birds flying.*)

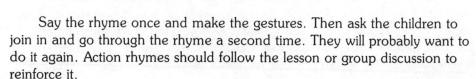

For happy children everywhere,
(*Clap hands lightly.*)

And for God's daily, loving care.
(*Heads bowed and hands folded.*)

Say the rhyme once and make the gestures. Then ask the children to join in and go through the rhyme a second time. They will probably want to do it again. Action rhymes should follow the lesson or group discussion to reinforce it.

Class Prayer

Many classes enjoy composing and saying their own prayers during the Thanksgiving season. Composing prayers provides a change from the usual classroom prayer. The prayers reflect the ideas of the students and are meaningful to them.

A class prayer can be one of thanksgiving to tie in with the holiday. The teacher should write the first part of the prayer on the blackboard. Or, if several classes share a room at different times, the prayer can be printed on poster board. The students are encouraged to complete the prayer by offering ideas that the teacher writes down.

A class prayer turns out like the following:

God, we thank you for

life

love

caring people

animals

health

friends.

If several classes compose prayers, collect the prayers in a booklet and duplicate it for each child. Students like to see what others have done. The prayers of other children give them ideas of things for which they can be thankful. The children can take the booklets home to share with their families and use as family prayers, mealtime prayers or private prayers.

We Thank You God Display

This project helps the children learn about God's many gifts to us by making individual displays of things for which they thank God. The children take the displays home as a reminder of the Thanksgiving season.

This is a simple craft that uses supplies available in most classrooms. Each child needs a piece of 18″ x 6″ construction paper. Bright colors work well.

Show the children how to fold the paper into an accordion fold with four sections. First, fold the strip of paper in half. Then make one more fold halfway on each side, folding in the opposite direction as the initial fold. This makes a four section display that stands up by itself.

Have the children label the top: *We Thank You, God.* For young children, print the words on the board for them to copy.

Then have the children label the bottom: *for people, for food, for animals, for flowers.* Thin markers make the words colorful.

Next, have the children select magazine pictures that illustrate each category. Each child needs one picture of people, one of a favorite food, one of an animal, and one of flowers. The children should glue the pictures onto the corresponding section of their accordion fold. For young children, precut pictures and have them select the ones they like best. Otherwise searching through magazines for pictures and cutting them out could take the whole class period.

This craft project makes a colorful reminder for the children of God's many gifts to us. It will stand up on a child's desk or dresser at home. Because the children choose pictures they like, the display has personal meaning for them. Each time the children look at their display at home, they will be reminded of the many beautiful things that God gave us out of love.

Word Search

Word search puzzles have become very popular in recent years. They are easy to make and can be adapted to many different lessons. Children enjoy the challenge and feel a sense of accomplishment when they complete an activity such as a word search. Such activities help focus the children's attention on the meaning of Thanksgiving.

A word search features a group of letters with words hidden among them. For a Thanksgiving word search, feature words that will remind the children of gifts from God. Any number of words can be hidden in a word search. Spell words only left to right or top to bottom for young children. It is a good idea to list the words that the children are expected to find.

Thanksgiving Word Search
Circle five words that are gifts from God.
Answers are found below.

Answers: people, dogs, food, grass, sun

Children enjoy this type of activity and it reminds them of God's gifts. Word search puzzles can be duplicated for the entire class. Older children can make up their own word search puzzles and exchange them. They may also include words hidden diagonally, right to left or bottom to top.

This activity, like others, should not be used exclusively. Any activity becomes routine if it is used week after week. Variety is important in selecting learning activities for children.

Thanksgiving Mural

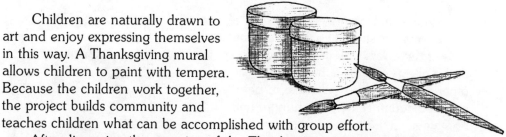

Children are naturally drawn to art and enjoy expressing themselves in this way. A Thanksgiving mural allows children to paint with tempera. Because the children work together, the project builds community and teaches children what can be accomplished with group effort.

After discussing the meaning of the Thanksgiving season with the children, help them make a mural. Lay out a long sheet of butcher paper so all the children have room to paint. Print the words *Thank you, God* in large letters in the middle of the mural before the children begin. Pour various colors of powdered tempera paint into several small plastic containers. Margarine containers work well. Mix some white with each color to make it bright. Also add water and mix in some dry laundry detergent so that the paint is easier to wash out if it accidentally gets on clothing. Encourage each child to paint a picture of something for which he or she is thankful.

When the mural is dry, hang it up as a reminder of the meaning of the Thanksgiving season. It also makes a great display behind the altar at a Thanksgiving prayer service. The children enjoy having their work displayed, and the mural helps them see Thanksgiving as a time to thank God.

Sponsor a Child

With Thanksgiving and thoughts of our many blessings should come greater awareness of those less fortunate. News reports tell of the effects of a drought or a hurricane or other natural disaster. We hear of people in war-torn countries who are hungry and homeless. Children need to become aware of our Christian responsibility to help others at home and in other parts of the world.

Sponsoring a child is one way to increase social awareness and to help a person in need. Television commercials and advertisements in magazines give information and addresses of organizations through whom this is done. For a set sum of money each month, a group is able to sponsor one particular child. Due to the money involved, this may be a joint venture of several classes. Explain the program to the children and the need for it. Let them vote on the country from which the sponsored child will be chosen.

The organization will send information and a picture of the child. The children will also be able to correspond with the child. The money will go to provide food, clothing, medical care and schooling for the sponsored child. Ask the children to contribute money from chores when they can. Send a letter home to the parents explaining the program.

This is an ongoing project, not a one-time thing. The contributions must be continued year round. This shows the children that caring about others in God's family is a continuing responsibility.

Horn of Plenty

We need to help the children become aware of the many different types of food that God created to keep us healthy and help us grow. A horn of plenty symbolizes God's many gifts to us, especially the food that we eat.

Have each child draw a horn of plenty shape on a sheet of brown construction paper. Provide several other colors of construction paper from which the children can cut various fruits and vegetables: red for apples and cherries, orange for carrots and oranges, purple for grapes and plums, yellow for lemons and bananas. The children may think of others. Have them glue the fruits and vegetables they select to the open end of the horn of plenty and print *Thank you, God* on the side.

This horn of plenty project provides a good opportunity for discussion about the many gifts which God has given to us. Remind the children that gifts are given to be shared. God expects all of us to share the food that comes from the earth. This is an important part of the Thanksgiving lesson.

Mealtime Grace

Most children have some type of Thanksgiving meal with their families. Many of them have a traditional Thanksgiving with turkey, stuffing, cranberry sauce and pumpkin pie. Thanksgiving is a good time to remind them that on this holiday—and all other days—it is only fitting that the meal begin with grace.

Explain that the grace can be in their own words or the standard table grace. It is a good idea to provide the children with a copy of this prayer to take home:

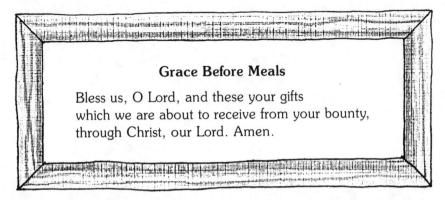

Grace Before Meals

Bless us, O Lord, and these your gifts
which we are about to receive from your bounty,
through Christ, our Lord. Amen.

Talk about the meaning of the words. Explain to the children that we ask God to bless us as a sign of our faith in him. Ask why we call our blessings from God gifts. If necessary, explain that it is because they are freely given to us out of God's love for us.

Many classes have some sort of Thanksgiving party in class. We can and should say thank you to God before we begin eating the treats. Say the grace before meals to show the children how to put into practice what has been discussed in class.

Table Prayer

Table prayers can help us feel in touch with God and the spirit of the season. Older children especially enjoy a table prayer such as the following which can be used at a parish gathering or at home during the Thanksgiving season:

Thank you, Lord,
>for the goodness of life around us:
>>for the beauty of the earth,
>>for each other,
>>for surprises and challenges.

Bless this meal,
>May it strengthen us
>>and lead us to a new awareness
>>of the goodness around us.

Most of all, may the strength we gain from this meal
>lead us to you,
>>the source of all goodness.

Amen.[3]

Blessings Book

The blessings book is a great project for the Thanksgiving season. It is a good follow-up to a class discussion of our many blessings. Only when children become aware of God's many gifts can they express thanks for them.

Ask each child in the class to draw a picture of something for which he or she is thankful. Using colorful markers, have them title the page *Thank you, God, for* at the top and sign it at the bottom.

As the children finish their thank-you pages, collect them in the blessings book, a three-ring binder with the cover decorated to make it attractive. Using felt for the cover and gluing felt flowers onto the front works well.

Bring the book forward at the class Thanksgiving Mass or prayer service. Place it in front of the altar at the preparation of the altar and the gifts as an outward sign of thankfulness for our many blessings. Explain to the children that God will see their book as he sees all that they do.

This project reinforces the lesson of Thanksgiving in a tangible way. It reminds the children that we need to say thank you to God for our many gifts at Thanksgiving time and always. It allows them to express to God what is in their hearts.

Thanksgiving Essays

Children need to think about what they are learning and express their feelings and ideas. Writing about the meaning of Thanksgiving affords children a time to focus their thoughts about this holiday.

Ask each child to write a short essay titled *What Thanksgiving Means to Me*. This is a good follow-up to a discussion of why we celebrate this American holiday. It provides an opportunity for each child to reflect on the meaning of the lesson in his or her own life.

Collect all the essays and have a volunteer type them in columns to make a Thanksgiving newsletter. Print each child's name after his or her essay. Title the paper *What Thanksgiving Means to Me* and duplicate a copy for each child to take home.

The essays turn out as individual as the children. Some write about food, others about relatives; some mention autumn leaves, others special customs. These essays personalize the Thanksgiving holiday and help children sort out what is really important about it.

Children like to see their essays "in print" and proudly take home their Thanksgiving newsletter to show parents and relatives. These essays also provide an opportunity for children to find out what other children think about Thanksgiving.

Thanksgiving Booklet

Making Thanksgiving booklets is a good project for younger children. This activity encourages the children to think about the many gifts we have from God.

Each time the class meets, ask the children to draw a picture for their booklets. The first page should be a picture of their families. The caption underneath should read *Thank you, God, for families*. The second page is for a drawing of their best friends. The caption underneath should read *Thank you, God, for friends*. On the third page, ask them to draw a picture of their favorite meal. The caption is *Thank you, God, for food*. The last page is for a picture of their pet or favorite animal. The bottom of this page should read *Thank you, God, for animals*.

Provide brightly colored markers for the children to use for their pictures. Reassure the children that there is no one right way to do this project. It is to be as individual as they are. Avoid holding up one child's work as an example to the others while they are working. Children can easily become discouraged.

The next step is for each child to make a construction paper cover for the booklet titled *My Thanksgiving Book by* (child's name). Then, help them assemble their pictures into the booklets using brads.

Art is a joyful way for children to give visual expression to their thoughts. Art projects help children to express their feelings in a way that is not limited by vocabulary. The children will also enjoy the favorable comments they receive when they bring home their booklets.

Ten Lepers Echo Pantomime

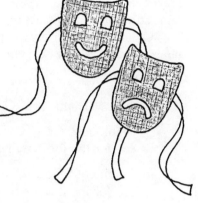

The bible story of the ten lepers who were healed by Jesus is a good reminder to say thank you to Jesus in our own lives.

Echo pantomime is a way of telling a bible story that involves the children. The teacher says a line and does a motion. The children echo the words and the motion. This continues throughout the story. An echo pantomime for the story of the Ten Lepers follows:

One day as Jesus was walking	(walk in place)
ten lepers called to him.	(hold up 10 fingers)
They begged Jesus	(fold hands together)
to make them better.	(fold arms across chest)
Jesus told them	(shake head yes)
to show themselves to the priest.	(point in distance)
On the way	(walk in place)
they saw that they were cured.	(look down)
One man ran back to Jesus	(run in place)
and thanked him.	(fold hands together)
Jesus said, "Ten were made better;	(hold up 10 fingers)
why has only one come back?"	(hands out, palms up)
Jesus told the man to go on his way,	(point in distance)
his faith had saved him.	(arms outstretched)

After the pantomime, talk with the children about things for which they are thankful. Help them relate this story to their own lives.

Sticker Prayer

This prayer idea for Thanksgiving time uses the popular self-stick stickers as illustrations. The children enjoy this project and they are reminded of our many blessings.

Older children should copy the following prayer from the bulletin board. Provide copies for younger children, perhaps in fancy printing such as calligraphy.

Thank You, God

Thank you, God,
    for the morning light.

Thank you, God,
    for the flowers so bright.

Thank you, God,
    for the food we eat.

Thank you, God,
    for the people we meet.

Thank you, God,
    for the birds that sing.

Thank you, God,
    for the love you bring. Amen.

To "frame" the prayer, have the children glue their paper to a larger, colorful sheet of construction paper. Then let them select six stickers to decorate their prayer which illustrate the key words. Stickers such as a sun, a flower, a fruit, a child, a bluebird, and a heart work well. These stickers are available at variety and card stores anywhere.

The stickers help the children concentrate on what the prayer is saying and remember it. They can take the prayer home and use it as a bedtime or a family prayer. Parents can read the prayer for the younger children, and the stickers will be reminders of some of the things for which the children can be thankful at Thanksgiving.

Psalm Prayer

The psalms are a wonderful source of prayers for the Thanksgiving season. This book of religious poetry speaks to our hearts as it surely did to people thousands of years ago.

Psalm 95, for example, can be used as a prayer at the beginning of class during Thanksgiving time. This psalm, like many, speaks of the glory of God our Creator.

The psalm should be read directly from the Bible, and the teacher should begin by explaining that it is a prayer from the Old Testament.

> Come, let us sing joyfully to the LORD;
>   let us acclaim the Rock of our salvation.
> Let us greet him with thanksgiving;
>   let us joyfully sing psalms to him.
> For the LORD is a great God,
>   and a great king above all gods;
> In his hands are the depths of the earth,
>   and the tops of the mountains are his.
> His is the sea, for he has made it,
>   and the dry land, which his hands have formed.
> Come, let us bow down in worship;
>   let us kneel before the LORD who made us.
> For he is our God,
>   and we are the people he shepherds, the flock he guides
>   (Ps 95:1-7).

Pause for a moment of silence after completing the reading of the psalm to allow individual contemplation.

Prayer Links

At Thanksgiving time we pause and remember our many blessings. The next step is to thank God for so blessing us.

Children can make a chain of prayer links to express to God their thankfulness. Each child in the class should pick out several one-inch strips of colorful construction paper to use. These can be precut easily before class using a paper cutter.

Encourage the children to think of one-sentence prayers of thanksgiving. Give them examples such as

> Thank you, God, for sunshine.
>
> Thank you, God, for pets.
>
> Thank you, God, for my grandparents.
>
> Thank you, God, for birthdays.

Ask them to write a prayer on each strip of paper.

When all the children have finished, have them assemble the prayer links into a colorful chain in any order they wish using tape. Hang the completed chain across the front of the room. The children's prayers of thanksgiving will be linked together in praise of God our Creator.

A prayer-link chain has a threefold purpose. First, it encourages the children to think of their blessings and give thanks. Second, it shows that their individual prayers are vital links holding the chain together. Third, it gives the children a sense of community with other Christians.

·2·

The Joy of

ADVENT

The word *Advent* means "coming." It is a time to prepare our hearts and our lives as we wait for the coming of Jesus. Advent is a time to renew in ourselves the joy that came into the world on that first Christmas. We focus on the promise that God made to his people and how that promise was fulfilled in Jesus. Advent is a time of hope.

During Advent we not only await the celebration of Jesus' coming into the world at Christmas, but we also look forward to his coming again at the end of time. While we are remembering the past, we are also anticipating the future. And that future is life with Jesus Christ.

We should use the season of Advent to get ready to live the message of Christmas. It is a time to share joy and hope with others by our caring and our love. We celebrate the love of God in sending us Jesus. We welcome the Lord into our lives.

During Advent we journey in faith toward the Messiah just as the Wise Men journeyed toward him following the star. Advent is the beginning of the liturgical year. It should also be a time for new beginnings for us as Christians.

Advent Candles

Advent candles remind us that the season of Advent is here. A large paper Advent wreath is a good bulletin board display during this time. If several classes share a room, the wreath can be glued to poster board and brought to class each week.

Use construction paper to make a paper Advent wreath and candles. Cut out three large purple candles and one large pink candle. Mark one purple candle *hope*, another *peace*, the third one *love*. Mark the pink candle *joy*. Also cut out four yellow flames and a large green wreath, or holly leaves that can be shaped into a wreath. Use purple letters to spell out *Advent*.

Put the wreath, candles and letters on the bulletin board or glue them to the poster board. Put a yellow flame above the candle marked hope. Save the remaining three flames.

Explain to the children that this Advent wreath will help them count the four weeks of Advent. Each candle stands for one week. Each week another candle will be "lit" with a paper flame to show that we are coming closer to Christmas. Light the pink candle for the third week.

Each week talk about the theme for that week: The first week, hope; the second week, peace; the third week, joy; the fourth week, love. The Advent wreath reminds the children to get ready for the coming of Jesus at Christmas. The presence of the Advent wreath will help them remember to give of themselves to others during this time. When all four candles are lit, the children will know that it is almost Christmas.

Angel Tree

Advent is a time to remember other people, especially children, who will not be receiving many gifts this Christmas. Due to unemployment or illness, some parents cannot afford to buy gifts for Christmas giving. Many times people in our parishes would open their hearts and buy a gift for a needy child if only they knew to whom to give. An angel tree makes this possible.

Many social agencies, public and private, know of people who are going without at Christmas time. Contact one of these agencies and ask for a list of children's names, ages, sizes and needs.

For each child's name on the list, cut out an angel shape from white poster board. This makes a sturdy ornament that will not tear. On the front of each angel print one child's first name and age. Use a red marker for girls and a green marker for boys. Outline the edge of the ornament with the marker to add a decorative touch.

On the back of each ornament list the child's clothing size and any special needs. Punch a hole in the top of each ornament and thread red or green yarn through it to make a hanger.

Hang the ornaments on an artificial Christmas tree placed where people will see it. An artificial tree is best because it does not present a fire

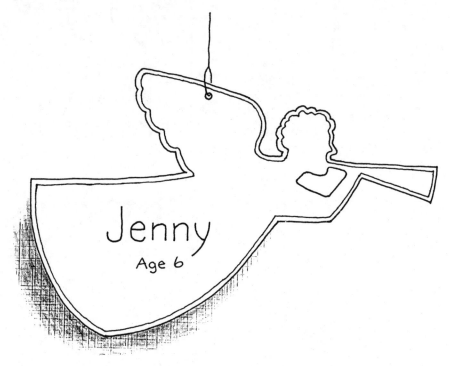

hazard. Also people are often willing to donate one to the church or school when they buy a new one for themselves.

Invite each family in the parish to take an angel from the tree and buy for that child. Let them know the deadline set by the sponsoring agency to bring the gifts. This is usually around the middle of December to allow time for distribution. Many times the agency will pick up the gifts at the church.

Ask the families to wrap the gifts and put the angel on the top for identification. The pile of gifts under the Christmas tree will brighten the holiday for many children. What better way to celebrate the coming of Jesus than by giving gifts to others in the name of his love!

Felt Hearts

During the Advent season we are to share with others the love that Jesus brought. The gift of love is not rightly received until it is shared with others. This is what love is all about. Hopefully this feeling of love for others that we show during Advent will overflow into our lives during other seasons.

A tangible way to help children understand that Advent is a time of love is to let them make felt hearts to use as Christmas tree ornaments. Hearts are recognized as a symbol of love even by very young children.

Red and green are good colors to use for ornaments. Provide a heart-shaped pattern to make it easier for the children to cut out hearts from the felt. Tell the children to also cut out a short strip of the same color to use as a hanger.

Provide a variety of trim and lace to use as decorations. Gold, green and red braid is sold by the yard at Christmas. Let each child choose a trim and glue it diagonally across the heart.

Be sure that each child's name is on masking tape on the back of the ornament. It is important that each of the children take home his or her own ornament for the family Christmas tree. These ornaments will serve year after year as a reminder of the love of the Advent season.

Joy Game

This board game helps children review facts about Advent and Christmas. It can be played by two to four players. It is an interesting way to help children recall details that enhance their understanding of the Christmas season and the Christmas story.

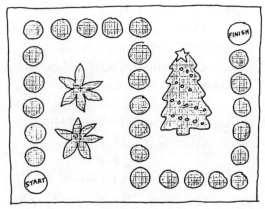

Construct the game board on paper or poster board. Make a path for the game tokens to follow by alternating 50 red and green self-adhesive circles. Place the circles up one side of the board, across the top, down the middle, across the bottom, and up the other side. Mark the bottom left-hand circle *start* and the top right-hand circle *finish*. Decorate the game board with self-stick Christmas stickers. Cover the board with clear self-sticking plastic for durability. Print each of the 20 questions and answers below on one side of an index card:

Question: In what town was Jesus born?
Answer: Bethlehem.

Question: What was the name of the cousin that Mary visited?
Answer: Elizabeth.

Question: Who were Jesus' first visitors?
Answer: Shepherds.

Question: How many weeks are there in Advent?
Answer: Four.

Question: What two words come after "Silent night" in the song of that name?
Answer: Holy night.

Question: Who was the mother of Jesus?
Answer: Mary.

Question: What shone in the skies over Bethlehem the night Jesus was born?
Answer: A star.

Question: Which gospel tells the story of the three wise men?
Answer: Matthew.

Question: On what date do we celebrate Jesus' birthday?
Answer: December 25.

Question: What was the name of Mary's husband?
Answer: Joseph.

Question: Who told the shepherds the good news of Jesus' birth?
Answer: The angels.

Question: Why did Mary and Joseph travel to Bethlehem?
Answer: For the census.

Question: Who followed the star to find Jesus?
Answer: The three Wise Men.

Question: What four words come after "Joy to the world" in that song?
Answer: The Lord is come.

Question: What is the feast of the three Wise Men called?
Answer: Epiphany.

Question: Which gospel tells the Christmas story?
Answer: Luke.

Question: What was the name of the angel who visited Mary?
Answer: Gabriel.

Question: What do we call the holiday on which we celebrate the birthday of Jesus?
Answer: Christmas.

Question: What gifts did the Wise Men bring to Jesus?
Answer: Gold, frankincense and myrrh.

Question: What did the Wise Men follow to find Jesus?
Answer: A star.

Place the question and answer cards in a pile face down. Many of the questions contain hints to answers of other questions so that players who listen carefully will do well.

Have the players take turns rolling a die and moving their tokens along the path from start to finish. When a player lands on a red space, the person on the left asks the question on the top card. For a correct answer, the player goes ahead one additional space. For an incorrect answer, the player remains on the same space until the next turn. Play continues until one player lands on or passes finish and wins the game.

This game is a fun way for the children to review information about Advent and Christmas. Children enjoy the challenge and excitement of board games. Games keep the interest of the children and help them learn and remember.

Holly Wreath

A wreath is a traditional symbol of the Christmas season. The circular shape reminds us that God's love has no beginning and no end. The green symbolizes God's everlasting love for us.

Paper holly wreaths are simple craft projects for children to make during the Advent season. The children are proud to take these wreaths home and use them as decorations.

The base for the holly wreath is a large paper plate with the inside circle cut out, leaving only the rim. Provide a pattern for the children to use to cut green construction paper holly leaves for their wreaths. Two leaves can be cut at once which makes this project go faster. Fifteen holly leaves are needed for each wreath.

The children should turn their paper rims over with the curved side out and glue the leaves onto it. Each leaf should slightly overlap the one before until the rim is completely covered by green holly leaves.

Then have the children cut out large red construction paper bows and glue one to the top of each wreath. Small red paper circles for holly berries provide the finishing touch.

The wreaths are lovely decorations that can be taped to a door, mirror or window at home as a reminder of the holiday season. Making holiday decorations enables children to participate in holiday plans and share the joy they feel during Advent.

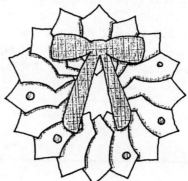

Nativity Ornament

An inexpensive way to make Christmas tree ornaments is to use discarded Christmas cards. Collect cards after Christmas to use the following year.

Use only Christmas cards with a nativity scene on them. Provide large drinking glasses to use as patterns for circles. Show the children how to put the glass on the card they have selected and draw around it with a pencil. Provide scissors so that they can cut out their circle. Pinking shears make a nice edge.

Next, have the children cut out a larger green or red circle from construction paper to use as a frame. Let them glue the picture circles onto the colored circles, then punch a hole through the top of the paper circle and string a length of red or green yarn through it. This makes a hanger for the ornament.

Because each Christmas card scene is different, each child's ornament will be different. These ornaments show the children how to use something discarded to make something new. The nativity scene on the ornaments help children remember that we have Christmas to celebrate only because Jesus came into the world on that first Christmas.

The children can print their name and the year on the back of the ornament and take it home for the family Christmas tree.

Advent Prayer

We must remember that we need God's help in all that we do. During Advent we ask his help as we get ready to celebrate the birthday of Jesus. Prayer is an important part of this preparation. Use the following prayer during the Advent season or write your own.

Dear God,
    We are getting ready to celebrate the birthday of your Son, Jesus. We ask your help to prepare our hearts for his coming. Fill us with joy as we prepare to receive this greatest of all gifts.
    Help us to remember those who are lonely this holiday season. Let us reach out to them and to others in our lives. Help us to take one step to make the world a better place to welcome your Son. May we witness to the love he brings into our lives and share that love with others.
    We ask this is the name of your Son, Jesus Christ.
Amen.

Prayer is an essential part of any holiday preparation and celebration; it is toward God that we must direct our lives and all our actions.

Tree Card

Children like to make their own greeting cards at Christmas time. Cards are a special way to share the joyful news of the Advent season.

Tree cards are simple to make with red and green self-adhesive circles. These are the kind sold to mark file folders. Also provide red and green construction paper with which to make the cards, a half-sheet for each card. Tell the children to fold their papers in half to make a greeting card.

Show the children how to make a tree on the front with the red and green circles. A red tree can stand on the front of a green card or vice versa. Or the children can use red and green circles on the same tree. Each child will need 16 circles: 15 to make a triangular-shaped tree and one circle for the trunk.

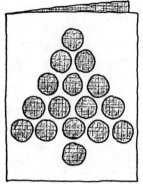

The children can then print a verse on the inside of their cards, a simple *Merry Christmas* or a greeting of their choice. The last step is to sign the card and give it to someone special. These cards are made and presented with love, and that is what the Advent season is all about.

Baby Food Collection

To be Christian means to care about others in our world. We must encourage children to help others in the name of Jesus whose birthday we celebrate at this time of year. We must not only show them that this is important, but provide ways for them to help. Caring is something that needs to be practiced, not just discussed.

It seems especially appropriate during Advent to collect baby food because Jesus Christ came into the world as a baby. A baby food collection is a good project because food pantries are always in need of baby food, juice and cereal. Some groups will also take used baby clothing and blankets.

Before beginning any collection, check with the food pantries or organizations that distribute baby food and nursery items in the community. Find out what their specific needs are and arrange for a date and time for delivery. Then send home a note with the children asking for baby food. Invite the whole parish to contribute. Provide clearly marked collection boxes in the hallway where people can leave their gifts.

Encourage the children to notice other needs in their community and in the world. Stress that giving and caring are not a one-time project, but something to continue throughout life.

Framed Greeting

Children like to make Christmas decorations to display at home. A framed greeting using a paper plate is an inexpensive idea for a holiday gift. These greetings can be as individual as their creators.

Provide bright red and green construction paper for the children. Encourage them to cut out a Christmas design; holly leaves, a Christmas tree, an ornament shape, a candle, a wreath and a bell are some ideas that can be used. Provide Christmas stencils or patterns for children who choose to use them.

Each child should then glue the Christmas decoration onto the center of a large paper plate. In a circle around the design he or she can print a Christmas greeting. Red and green markers give it a holiday touch. The greeting can be whatever the child chooses, for example, "Christmas greetings to one and all" or "Rejoice because Jesus has come." Young children may want to repeat a short greeting such as "Merry Christmas" over and over.

To hang up the designs, the children can punch a hole in the top of the paper plate and thread a length of red or green yarn through it. The edge of the paper plate forms a frame for the decoration. Suggest that they take these home to give to someone special.

Wrapping Paper

Children like to make things themselves to give to others with love. During Advent children often make Christmas gifts for their parents in class. These gifts become extra special when wrapped in handmade wrapping paper.

Here is a simple and inexpensive way to make beautiful wrapping paper with white tissue paper and food coloring. Each child should take a single sheet of tissue paper and fold it in half several times. Six folds makes the paper into a small square. It need not be folded in any certain way.

Set up two bowls for food coloring. In one bowl mix one part red food coloring with two parts water. Do the same in another bowl with green food coloring and water.

Instruct the children to dip the corners of their tissue squares into the food coloring. Two opposite corners should be dipped into red, and the other two corners into green. Caution the children not to dip their papers too deeply into the food coloring or the colors will run together.

Allow the folded papers to dry for a minute or so. Then very carefully and slowly unfold the tissue to reveal the lovely design. Each sheet of wrapping paper is unique and displays the traditional Christmas colors of red and green. Allow the paper to dry on newspaper until near the end of class. The children can wrap their gifts in this very special handmade wrapping paper.

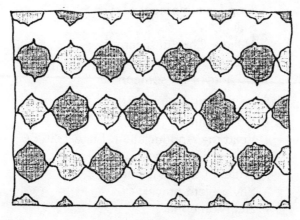

Advent Calendar

Advent is a time to get ready to welcome Jesus. The Advent calendar helps children learn how they can prepare for the coming of Jesus at Christmas.

An Advent calendar not only helps the children know how long it is until Christmas, but if each day has an appropriate suggestion it can help them get ready. The children can take their calendars home and thus extend the learning beyond the classroom.

To make an Advent calendar, draw a square for each day of Advent and mark the date in the upper left hand corner. In each square print a suggestion for an appropriate activity. (Suggestions are found below.) Try to make the activities ones that the children can do with a minimum of adult help. Title the page *My Advent Calendar* and duplicate one for each child. Suggestions are:

FIRST WEEK OF ADVENT:
> Tell someone you love him or her.
> Pray the Our Father.
> Stop for a moment of silence.
> Say grace.
> Make a Christmas card.
> Thank God for someone special.
> Do a favor for someone.

SECOND WEEK OF ADVENT:
> Go to church.
> Read the Annunciation, Luke 1:26-56.
> Forgive someone.
> Write a Christmas poem.
> Say a silent prayer.
> Help someone.
> Donate to a toy collection.

THIRD WEEK OF ADVENT:
        Sing a Christmas carol.
        Make an ornament.
        Say a morning prayer.
        Hug your parents.
        Share your time with someone.
        Say hello to a neighbor.
        Ask God's help.

FOURTH WEEK OF ADVENT:
        Pray for missionaries who bring the good news.
        Give a gift.
        Read the Christmas story, Luke 2:1-20.

In addition to the calendar, give each child an envelope with self-stick gold stars. Ask the children to do as many of the activities as they can to get ready for Jesus. When they complete an activity, they can put a gold star in the upper right-hand corner of the day's square. Assure them that they do not have to do all of the activities, but encourage each child to do at least one. It is helpful to do some of the activities in class. Encourage the children to light the way to Christmas with the stars on their calendars.

Sticker Calendar

Advent seems very long to young children as they wait eagerly for Christmas to come. A class sticker calendar for Advent helps children see that the time of waiting is getting shorter as Christmas nears. This is a good idea for classes that meet daily.

Draw a class Advent calendar on poster board. Be sure each day has a large square with the date marked on it. Do not mark past December 25; this shows that Christmas is the focus of Advent. Include the days of November that fall within Advent. Mark the calendar *Advent Calendar* at the top and put it on the bulletin board where all the children can see it.

Explain to the children that Advent is the time of waiting and getting ready for Christmas. The Advent calendar will show them how long it is until Christmas.

Purchase colorful Christmas stickers for the calendar, one for each day of Advent. Christmas stickers can be found in variety and card stores everywhere.

At the beginning of class each day select one child to choose a sticker and place it on the current day's date. Be sure that all the children get a turn during Advent.

Use the class Advent calendar to remind the children that during Advent they should be getting ready in their hearts to welcome Jesus.

Advent Poem

Help the children understand the season of
Advent by writing a class poem. A good poetry form
to use with a group is the diamente, a seven-line
poem with a specific form: one noun, two adjectives,
three gerunds, four nouns, three gerunds, two
adjectives, one noun. The words in a diamente form a diamond shape.

After talking with the children about the meaning of Advent, work with
them on a poem. As the children suggest words, print them on the chalkboard or a sheet of poster board. The first noun in the poem should be
Advent. An Advent diamente turns out this way:

Advent

hopeful   joyful

waiting   sharing   caring

trees   candles   wreaths   stockings

praying   bringing   helping

bright   cheerful

love

This type of Advent poem helps capture the spirit of the season. Display the poem in the classroom throughout Advent as a reminder of what
the season is all about.

·3·

The Message of
CHRISTMAS

Christmas is a season to reflect on what it means to follow Jesus Christ. He showed us a way of life that enables us to be all that we were created to be.

As teachers of God's love we must help children understand that at Christmas we are celebrating the birth of Jesus and all that his coming means to us.

We are to bring Christ into the world for others. We must witness to his love in our lives. We must make his presence felt not only during the Christmas season, but throughout the year.

Christmas should fill our minds with joy and our hearts with love. We are to share that love with others in Jesus' name. This is how we truly celebrate his birth—by remembering and living what he taught us.

The coming of Jesus Christ on that first Christmas is the greatest gift the Father has given us. He gave his only Son that we might have life everlasting. This gift is to be shared with others, for Jesus came into the world for all people and all time. We are to make the Son visible in the world to others by living what he taught.

Chrismon Tree

A Chrismon tree is a beautiful offering to God, a tree decorated with symbols that represent Christ. *Chrismon* is a combination of two words—*Christ* and *monogram*. A Chrismon tree tells the good news of Christ.[1]

Many different symbols can be used. Some of them are:

Chi Rho—the first letters of Christ in the Greek alphabet

Star—symbol of the birth of Jesus

IHS—the first letters of Jesus in Greek

Crown—symbol of the kingship of Jesus

Chrismons are white and gold ornaments. White represents our Lord's perfection, and gold his glory. Styrofoam, satin balls, sequins, pearls, gold metal beads, mesh, glitter and other materials can be used in the construction of Chrismons.

Explain the meaning of the symbols so the children understand the significance of the tree.

The Chrismon tree certainly helps us remember that Christ is the reason for Christmas.

Christmas Story

One way to help the children understand the story of the first Christmas is to show them a filmstrip like "Baby Born in a Stable" by Family Films (available from Augsburg Publishing House). This particular filmstrip tells the story so simply and completely that it is suitable even for very young children. A good filmstrip helps children picture the events of that long-ago first Christmas.

Note: Be sure you preview any filmstrip you select for suitability to your class' age level and to the material you wish to have emphasized.

Talk about the filmstrip afterward to clear up any misconceptions. Ask the children questions to see if they have the story clear in their minds. See if they can name the mother of Jesus, the town where Jesus was born, his first visitors. Talk about this special baby. Remind them that this child whose birthday we celebrate each year grew up to be a man called Jesus Christ, the Son of God, who taught all of us how to love God and others.

Christmas Stand-up

It sometimes seems easy to lose sight of what Christmas really means in all the hustle and bustle of preparations. Children can each make a Christmas stand-up to remind them of the true meaning of the season.

Cut sheets of red or green construction paper into four equal pieces. Give each child one of these pieces. Instruct them to fold the piece in half to form a self-standing card with the folded edge at the top.

Have each child print on the stand-up the bible verse which summarizes the meaning of Christmas: "A savior has been born." Print the reference, Luke 2:11, underneath the verse. Provide nativity stickers for the children to use to decorate the stand-ups. These are available at Christian book stores.

The children can take their stand-ups home to display. Each time they see them, they will be reminded of the meaning of Christmas by the picture and words. The verse notation will enable them to look up the Christmas story in the Bible if they choose.

Glory Chain

We need to help children see Christmas as a time for praising God who sent Jesus to us. One way to remind them is by making a glory chain. This is a paper-link chain that spells out the words that the angels said on that first Christmas to the shepherds: "Glory to God in the highest."

Explain to the children that the angels were giving honor to God through these words. Talk to them about how we should praise God. Remind them that we use these words of the angels at Mass each time we begin the Gloria. Making a chain will help them remember these words.

Duplicate the words of the angels on brightly colored paper, each word on a different color. Leave a one-inch space between words. Cut the paper so that each word is on a strip about one-inch wide. Put each word in a different box in order of the verse; for example, the first box would have in it all the strips labeled "Glory."

Have each child assemble a paper chain with the words *Glory to God in the highest* in order. Use tape rather than glue to assemble the chain because it sticks right away. When finished, each child will have the angels' words on a brightly colored paper chain to take home.

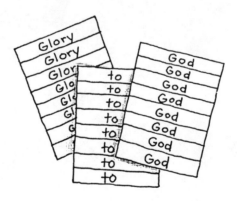

Jesus Is Born Echo Pantomime

Echo pantomime is a wonderful way to help children retell the Christmas story. The teacher says each line and performs the accompanying motion. The children then echo the words and actions.

Jesus Is Born[2]

Mary and Joseph went to Bethlehem	(walk in place)
to be counted in the census.	(count on fingers)
There was no room at the inn	(shake head)
so they stayed in a stable.	(point)
That night when all was quiet	(finger over lips)
Jesus was born.	(rock arms side to side)
Shepherds were in the fields	(point)
watching over their sheep.	(shield eyes with hand)
An angel came to them	(arms outstretched)
to tell them that Jesus was born.	(point)
The angels sang "Glory to God"	(hands cup mouth)
Then the shepherds went to Bethlehem	(walk in place)
to look for Jesus.	(look side to side)
They found him in the stable.	(shake head yes)
The shepherds went back to their sheep	(walk in place)
praising God for his gift.	(arms outstretched)

This echo pantomime is a good learning activity for young children. They do not need to be able to read to do it because they follow the teacher's lead. Since they participate in the telling of the story, they remember it longer. This is a joyful activity for a joyful time of year.

Round Robin

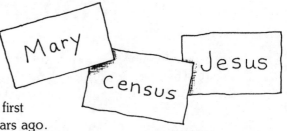

The story of the first Christmas is familiar to many children, and they enjoy helping to tell it again. A round robin retelling of the story also helps children remember what happened on that first Christmas almost two thousand years ago.

Sit in a circle with the children. The teacher begins the story with "Mary was a young girl living in the town of Nazareth." The turn passes to the left around the circle. Each child gets a chance to add a phrase to the telling of the Christmas story.

If the children in the class are hesitant about speaking out, provide cue cards. Print key words from the story on index cards and place one on each chair. Key words are *Mary, Gabriel, Elizabeth, census, Joseph, Bethlehem, inn, Jesus, shepherds, angels, stable,* and *flocks.* As the turn passes around the circle, each child tells the part of the story prompted by the cue card.

One advantage to using cue cards is that the children can tell the story over and over, changing seats each time so that they tell a different part of the story. This type of activity is a good change from simply reading the Christmas story to the children year after year. It involves the children in the learning and makes it interesting for them.

Star Tree

A special class project for Christmas time is the star tree. This bulletin-board decoration helps children remember that people, not trimmings, are the important part of Christmas. It features the name of each child in the class.

To make a star tree, cut a large green tree shape out of green poster board. A triangle with a square at the bottom for the trunk is simple and works well. Ask each child in the class to cut out a yellow star from construction paper. Provide a pattern for children who might have difficulty with this. Using green fine-line markers, have each child print his or her name on the star.

As the children finish, help them put their stars on the tree. A glue stick is quick and easy and does not soak through the paper. Put the stars on the tree in rows. The top of the tree should have one star, then a row with two, next a row with three stars, then four, then five, and so on, depending upon how many children are in the class.

This project helps the children feel that they are a special part of the Christmas season.

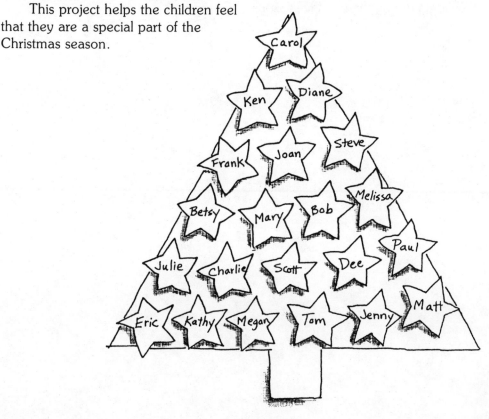

Christmas Book

Children love for their teachers to read to them. A library of children's books is important in the religious education of children. Books can sometimes speak to children in a way nothing else can. Always select a story to read aloud which reinforces the theme of the lesson.

A good storybook for young children at Christmas time should be short enough to keep their interest and attention. The story of the first Christmas should be told in a simple way that children can follow. Colorful pictures can help children visualize the story.

It is important to read books to children. Storybooks written in their language help reinforce the message of Christmas for children. Books can reach into children's minds and hearts and help them learn about God's love.

See the annotated bibliography, pages 149-151, for books to read to children during the holiday seasons.

People Game

A fun activity for primary children is the Christmas people game. Children like to play games and this one helps them remember the names of people in the Bible who were part of the first Christmas. The game is played by two children. It can be used as a before-class activity for early arrivals or as one activity in a series of learning centers.

To make the game cards, cut six index cards in half. On each card print one of the names and descriptions below. Then make a duplicate set.

MARY
mother of Jesus

SHEPHERDS
Jesus' first visitors

JESUS
born on Christmas day

ELIZABETH
cousin of Mary

JOSEPH
foster father of Jesus

ANGELS
announced the good news

The children first mix up the cards. Then they set them out face down in four rows of three cards each. The children take turns turning over two cards and trying to select matches.

If the two cards do not match, they are put back face down and the play passes to the other child. If the two cards do match, the child removes them from the game and takes another turn. The children try to remember where they have seen each card. The game can be played over and over because each time it is played the cards are in different places.

Christmas Stationery

Young children like to give gifts as well as receive them. In our classrooms we can help children learn that the best gifts come from the heart. A personal message written by a child for someone special in his or her life is this kind of gift. We can help children learn to give of themselves in this way through Christmas stationery.

To make Christmas stationery, simply draw a shape associated with Christmas on a standard sheet of typing paper. Use a ruler to draw lines within the shape on which the children can print or write. You may use a variety of shapes: a bell, a star, a gift box, holly, a Christmas tree. Duplicate the pages for the children.

Let the children choose the shape on which they want to write their message. Encourage them to write to someone special in their life and tell that person their feelings. Remind the children to sign their names. If some children want to write more than one note, allow them to do so. That way they won't have to choose between people they love.

Provide envelopes in which the children can put their Christmas messages. Tell them to put the name of the person for whom the message is intended on the outside. Also give each child a Christmas sticker to put on his or her envelope for a festive touch. Then the children can take home their envelopes and put them under the tree until Christmas morning.

Christmas Tape

A Christmas memories tape is a good activity for younger children at Christmas time. Children enjoy telling others about their ideas and what they like about Christmas. A tape recording helps children feel important and that others want to hear what they have to say.

Seat the children in a circle on the floor or around a table. Put the tape recorder in the middle. Have the children go around the circle and one by one tell what they like about Christmas. Ask them to begin by saying their name and then complete this sentence: "I like Christmas because . . ." Some children will need prompting. Others will mention several things. Teachers should participate also; children like to have their teachers be a part of things. When all the children have had a turn, play the tape back for the class to hear.

Children like to hear themselves and their friends on tape. Making a tape helps children personalize the Christmas lesson and what it means in their own lives. It also provides the opportunity for children to learn about Christmas traditions and celebrations by listening to other children. A Christmas tape helps children to feel the joyful spirit that is a part of Christmas.

Legend of the Poinsettia

The bright red poinsettia has become a Christmas tradition in many homes and churches. These tropical plants lend a festive touch to the Christmas season. Many of the children will remember these plants from prior years. Tell the children the lovely legend of the poinsettia and why it is seen at Christmas.

It was Christmas Eve. A little girl who lived in a town in Mexico wanted to bring a present to the Christ Child in the creche scene at her church. All of her friends were bringing him gifts, but the little girl did not have any money to buy a gift. Her family was poor.

On the way to church that night she gathered some green weeds from the edge of a field. She brought the bouquet to the church, walked up the center aisle with the others, and laid her small gift by the creche.

Suddenly, the legend says, the green weeds turned a beautiful red. A miracle had taken place because the little girl had given a wonderful gift to the Christ Child—the gift of her love.

Many churches use these red poinsettia plants near the altar at Christmas to remind all of us that the best gift we can give is the gift of love.

Paper Poinsettia

Children like to make paper poinsettias at Christmas to decorate their classrooms. These traditional Christmas flowers make lovely window decorations. Each child can make one.

For each paper poinsettia use one sheet of red construction paper. Using a black marker, outline three double sets of leaves. (Three pieces of paper are easier to work with than six individual petals.) The children should carefully cut around the black line, leaving some red showing around the edges.

Next, have the children glue the three sets of leaves together, one on top of another so that all six show. Show them how to use a black marker to draw veins on the leaves to give them a more three-dimensional look.

The final touch is to form the center of each poinsettia with glitter. The easiest way to do this is to put the paper poinsettia in a box lid. Put glue in a circle in the center of the flower. Carefully sprinkle on gold glitter. Shake off the excess, being sure that all the glitter remains in the box. This makes cleanup simple.

Put a piece of double-sided tape on the back of each poinsettia and attach it to a window, bulletin board or wall. The poinsettias give the classroom area a festive look. Each child will be proud to see his or her poinsettia displayed.

Caroling

At Christmas we share our joy at Christ's coming with others. One way to do this is to go caroling at a nursing home. Many nursing home residents never leave their place of residence during this holy season. Thus we must bring the spirit of Christmas to them.

Arrangements for caroling must be made at the nursing home in advance. One of the best ways to carol is to go down each hall of the nursing home singing traditional carols. This reaches people who do not come out of their rooms for programs that are held in the community room. Some people are shy, others may be in ill health. By caroling in the halls, all of the residents will be able to hear the carols. In this way we can reach out and touch others with the Christmas spirit.

Take time to stop in the doorways of residents' rooms and wish them a Merry Christmas after a carol is completed. This adds a personal touch. Many nursing home residents have very few visitors and are especially delighted to see children. Traditional carols are familiar to both elderly people and children. Musical accompaniment is not necessary. One verse of each carol is best, since many children are not familiar with the second verses. Good carols are:

Away in a Manger
Silent Night
The First Noel
Joy to the World
O, Come, All Ye Faithful
It Came Upon a Midnight Clear
O Little Town of Bethlehem
Hark the Herald Angels Sing

These songs can be sung over and over as the carolers move down the halls. The words speak the true message of Christmas to all who hear them.

Christmas Banner

Making a Christmas banner is a way to share the joy and hope of the Christmas season with others. Banners are a meaningful way to express the spirit of Christmas; they speak to all who pass by of the presence of Jesus in our midst.

Making a large Christmas banner for the church vestibule or classroom hallway allows students to work together as a community to welcome Jesus into their hearts. A Christmas banner helps students express what Christmas means in a visible and tangible way.

A Christmas banner is usually composed of a word or words, perhaps *joy* or *rejoice,* and symbols such as a manger or a star.

Felt letters and symbols glued onto a burlap background in a neutral color make a nice banner. Craft glue works best and does not soak through the felt. Stitch a rod pocket through the top and thread a wooden dowel through it. Tie craft yarn to the ends of the dowel and hang the banner on a nail or hook.

A banner is a good way to remind everyone that Christmas is indeed a special celebration. It is a time when we express to others what it means to be a Christian. It is a time to remember that God has given us the greatest gift of all, Jesus.

Christmas Pageant

This Christmas pageant tells the story of Christmas. It uses the biblical account of the birth of Jesus and well-known carols. The events are acted out, but there are no lines to memorize because a narrator reads the Christmas story and a speaking choir reads the parts of the characters as the actors perform appropriate gestures. A singing choir sings Christmas carols for the program.[3]

Provide simple costumes for the characters. Gather some props such as a lifelike doll, a manger bed, staffs for the shepherds, and the like. Plan for two rehearsals.

As the people are arriving, play "O, Come, All Ye Faithful." Use a tape or record if you don't have a piano.

NARRATOR: The story of Christmas began long, long ago when God promised to send the Savior. The chosen people of Israel waited thousands of years for that Savior to come. The prophets kept that hope alive. They reminded the people that God would keep his promise.

SPEAKING CHOIR: "Therefore the Lord himself will give you this sign: the virgin shall be with child, and bear a son, and you shall name him Immanuel."

SINGING CHOIR: "O Come, O Come, Emmanuel" (one verse)

NARRATOR: God chose Mary, a young girl who lived in the town of Nazareth in Galilee, to be the mother of his Son. Mary was engaged to a man named Joseph of the house of David. (*Enter Mary and sit on a stool.*) God sent the angel Gabriel to ask Mary to be the mother of the Savior. (*Enter Gabriel and stand a short distance from Mary.*)

SPEAKING CHOIR: "Rejoice, O highly favored daughter! The Lord is with you. Blessed are you among women. . . . You have found favor with God. You shall conceive and bear a son and give him the name Jesus. . . . He will be called Son of the Most High . . . and his reign will be without end."

NARRATOR: Mary was afraid, but she said yes to God.

SPEAKING CHOIR: "I am the servant of the Lord. Let it be done to me as you say." (*Exit Mary and Gabriel.*)

NARRATOR: "In those days Caesar Augustus published a decree ordering a census of the whole world. . . . Everyone went to register, each to his own town. And so Joseph went from the town of Nazareth in Galilee to Judea, to David's town of Bethlehem—because he was of the house and lineage of David—to register with Mary, his espoused wife, who was with child." (*Mary and Joseph walk slowly across stage. They sit on either side of the manger.*)

NARRATOR: "While they were there . . . she gave birth to her first-born son and wrapped him in swaddling clothes and laid him in a manger, because there was no room for them in the place where travelers lodged." (*Mary lifts up the doll from the manger and cradles it as Joseph looks on.*)

SINGING CHOIR: "Away in a Manger" (one verse)

NARRATOR: "There were shepherds in that region, living in the fields and keeping night watch by turns over their flocks. The angel of the Lord appeared to them as the glory of the Lord shone around them, and they were very much afraid." (*Enter shepherds with staffs, then angel.*)

SPEAKING CHOIR: "You have nothing to fear! I come to proclaim good news to you—tidings of great joy to be shared by the whole people. This day in David's city a savior has been born to you, the Messiah and Lord. Let this be a sign to you: in a manger you will find an infant wrapped in swaddling clothes."

NARRATOR: "Suddenly, there was with the angel a multitude of the heavenly host, praising God."

SINGING CHOIR: "Hark the Herald Angels Sing" (one verse)

NARRATOR: "When the angels had returned to heaven, shepherds said to one another":

SPEAKING CHOIR: "Let us go over to Bethlehem and see this event which the Lord has made known to us."

NARRATOR: "They went in haste and found Mary and Joseph, and the baby lying in a manger; once they saw, they understood what had been told them concerning this child." (*Shepherds walk over to Mary, Joseph and manger*).

SINGING CHOIR: "O Little Town of Bethlehem" (one verse)

NARRATOR: "The shepherds returned, glorifying and praising God for all they had heard and seen." (*Shepherds leave.*) Today we come to praise the Christ Child as did those shepherds long ago. We also tell others the good news that the angels told them: Jesus Christ is the gift from God to all of us.

NARRATOR: Let us stand and sing "Joy to the World."

(*The end.*)

This type of pageant reminds us of what it is that we celebrate this time of year. It focuses our attention on the true meaning of Christmas as a celebration of the birth of Jesus Christ and speaks to our hearts of the joy of Christmas.

The Story of Epiphany

Epiphany, one of the oldest feasts of the church, commemorates the visit of the Magi to the child Jesus as recounted in the gospel of Matthew. It reminds us that we are to follow Jesus' star in our own lives.

The Magi show us that Jesus came for all people; they represent all people who were not Jewish.

Read to the children the biblical account of the visit of the Magi, Matthew 2:1-12. Discuss the story with the children. Ask questions to ascertain their understanding and promote discussion such as:

What did the Wise Men follow?

Whom did they ask about Jesus?

What did they bring to give to Jesus?

Ask the children what this story means for their lives. Remind them that Jesus came for everyone and that everyone is to look for Jesus in his or her life.

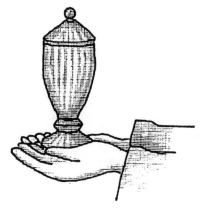

Wise Men Echo Pantomime

One way to help children learn about the coming of the Wise Men is an echo pantomime. The teacher says each line and does the accompanying motion. The children repeat the words and actions. The following echo pantomime follows the biblical account of the Wise Men's visit.

When Jesus was born	(cradle arms)
wise men saw a bright star.	(point up)
They knew in their hearts	(hand over heart)
that this was good news.	(shake head yes)
They set out on a long journey	(walk in place)
to find the special child.	(cross arms over chest)
They went to Jerusalem	(walk in place)
to ask about Jesus.	(cradle arms)
Then they went on to Bethlehem	(walk in place)
following the shining star.	(point up)
The wise men looked for Jesus	(shield eyes, look around)
Until at last they found him.	(shake head yes)
They offered him gifts	(palms up)
of gold, frankincense and myrrh.	(count on three fingers)
The wise men thanked God	(bow head, fold hands)
that Jesus came for everyone.	(hold arms outstretched)

This echo pantomime helps children understand the story of Epiphany. It helps them remember that Jesus came for all of us.

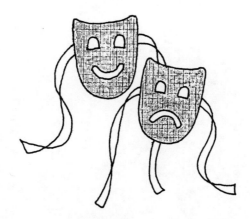

Star Puzzle

The feast of Epiphany reminds all of us to follow Jesus' star in our lives. We too should honor him and seek his presence.

Star puzzles are reminders that we are to seek Jesus as the Magi did. To make star puzzles, have each child cut out two large yellow stars from construction paper. Provide a pattern for them to use. One star is for the puzzle itself and the other for the backing when the puzzle is assembled.

Ask the children to print *We have followed his star* on one of their stars. The words should be spaced out so that each one is near one of the points of the star. Next, show the children how to cut up their stars into puzzles of five pieces each. Each piece should have one of the words on it.

Have the children mix up their five puzzle pieces and see if they can reassemble them with the words in the right order. Be sure they do not get their pieces mixed up with those of another child. When all the children have put together their star puzzles, tell them to glue the pieces onto the backing star so they will have a completed star to take home.

Star Poem

A star poem is written in the shape of a star and contains thoughts or images about the visit of the Magi to Jesus. It helps focus the thoughts of the children on the meaning of the feast of Epiphany in their own lives. Use a star poem to reinforce the lesson about the Magi.

Provide an outline of a star on a piece of paper for each child. Also give each child a blank sheet of typing paper to put over the outline. The children print words going around the star that relate to Epiphany. They need as many words or phrases as it takes to completely go around the star one time. When they finish and remove the star outline, they will have a star poem.

A star poem is a series of reflections. The phrases do not need to rhyme or form complete sentences. Ask the children to answer two questions in their poem: What happened at Epiphany? and What does that have to do with our lives?

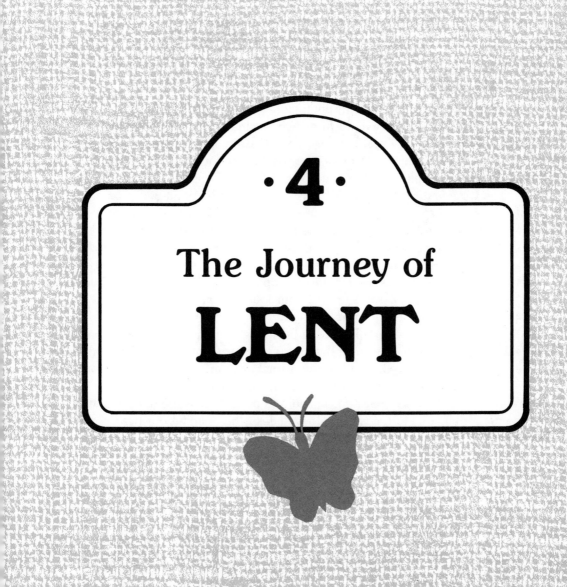

·4·

The Journey of
LENT

Lent offers us a time of reflection to see where we are on our journey with God. It offers us an opportunity to take positive steps along our life path and to grow in faith, hope and love.

Each lenten journey mirrors in a small way our lifetime journey with God. It may not always be easy, but we still are responsible for directing our lives along his path. We must trust God to guide us and be with us on our journey through Lent and through life.

The 40 days of Lent extend from Ash Wednesday to Easter Sunday. They symbolize the 40 days that Jesus spent fasting in the desert in preparation for his public ministry. Sundays are not included in this count because each Sunday is a celebration of the first Easter and Christ's resurrection.

The word *lent* means "spring." It is significant that spring brings longer and longer days at a time when we are turning away from ourselves and toward the light of God. Lent is a time for reflection, prayer, growth and learning. It is a time to follow in the footsteps of Christ.

In order to help children learn about following Jesus Christ we must help them learn what God wants of his people. Prayer is an important part of this process; it is an essential part of our journey. We must provide opportunities for children to pray during Lent.

In order to know about Jesus, we have to study scripture. The gospels are especially important because the words and deeds of Jesus are recorded there. As Christians, we are to live the gospel message. It is for this reason that on Ash Wednesday the priest makes the sign of the cross on our foreheads and says "Turn away from sin and be faithful to the gospel." Lent is a time for all of us to focus on following Jesus by opening our hearts to his presence in the world and in our lives.

On our journey through Lent we must walk with God. As God's people we must search for his call in our lives and follow it. We need to help children discover what it means to live as Christians through ideas and activities which are meaningful in their lives.

Lenten Pledge

Making a pledge at the beginning of Lent each year is a long-standing tradition. A lenten pledge is a promise that is kept during the period of Lent. It is meant to bring us closer to God and to help us to do his will in our lives.

Explain to the children that in order to follow Jesus we must follow his example. Ask them to think of things that they can do in their own lives to act as Jesus wants. Some possible suggestions are: to learn a new prayer, to help someone with chores, to smile at someone every day, to invite a lonely child to play, to say grace before meals, to pray for those who are ill.

Ask each child to pick a lenten pledge. It need not be one mentioned in class. Then ask the children to think of one word that summarizes the pledge, for example, pray, share, help, smile, care.

Give each child a sheet of purple paper. Ask them to draw the shape of their foot on the paper by tracing around one of their shoes. At the top of the paper they should write *My lenten pledge is to*. Inside the foot shape each child should write his or her individual pledge.

Ask the children to take their lenten pledges home as a reminder to follow in the footsteps of Jesus during Lent. Tell them to do their best, but also assure them that God doesn't expect them to be perfect. As Easter approaches remind them occasionally that they should still be working on their lenten pledges.

Lent Letters

Another way children can make lenten pledges is by writing Lent letters to God.[1] This activity calls for thought about the meaning of Lent and how the spirit of the season can be carried out in the child's life.

Invite the children to share their thoughts and ideas with God by writing a letter. Ask the children to think carefully about an activity they can carry out that will help them develop a closer relationship with God.

Provide paper and envelopes so that each child can write a beginning-of-Lent letter that describes what he or she will try to do during Lent. Tell the students to use a regular letter form beginning with "Dear God" and ending with their signature. Remind them that their signature is their promise to do the best that they can in carrying out their chosen activity. When the letters are finished, the children should fold them, put them in envelopes and write *Dear God* on the front.

Tell the students that this Lent letter is between them and God unless they choose to share it with someone. Ask them to keep the envelopes where they will see them at home as a reminder of Lent and their promise.

Good Shepherd

A good reminder that we are to follow Jesus is the story of the Good Shepherd. This is a Bible story that can be used during Lent with young children.

Begin by explaining to the children that shepherds are people who care for sheep, watching over them and keeping them safe. They take the sheep out to where there is green grass for them to eat and water for them to drink. Sometimes the shepherds stay out all night with the sheep. Then they lead them back home. If one of the sheep gets lost, the shepherd goes out and looks until he finds it. Good shepherds care about their sheep.

Read aloud Jesus' description of the Good Shepherd (John 10:14-15). Explain to the children that the Father Jesus refers to is God. Tell them that Jesus described himself as a good shepherd so that we would know he always watches over us like the shepherd watches over his sheep. We are to follow Jesus, the Good Shepherd, as real sheep follow their shepherd.

To help the children remember the story, show them how to make a fluffy sheep to take home. Provide each child with a sheet of construction paper on which the outline of a large sheep has been traced. Title the paper *Jesus Is the Good Shepherd*. With glue and cotton balls, the children can fill in the outline to make a fluffy white sheep. They should put cotton balls all over the sheep except for the face and hooves. When the glue dries, they can pet their soft sheep.

Operation Rice Bowl

Fasting has been a traditional part of the lenten observance for many people. It is important that we see this as giving up something so that others may have what they need. One way to do this is to participate in Operation Rice Bowl. This program calls upon people to eat a reduced meal once a week during Lent and to contribute the money saved to help victims of poverty around the world. One person does make a difference. Together we can work wonders.

The money collected is used to help people increase local food production and provide water resources; to provide tools, seed and training in agriculture; to fund other development projects that help people help themselves. Thus the benefits of this program are long lasting.

Operation Rice Bowl provides cardboard containers for each participating family to use during Lent. The money collected is a concrete expression of our concern for those who suffer from poverty and hunger. The container on the family table during Lent is a strong reminder to children of our responsibility to share with others.

Prayer Candle

Prayer is an important part of being a Christian and an important part of Lent. A prayer candle helps the children remember to pray at mealtime during Lent.

Each child should bring a thick white candle from home. Provide silver sequins and straight pins so the children can decorate the front of their candles. Push the pins through the center of the sequins to secure them to the candle. It helps to use a thimble to push on the pins.

Suggest that children form symbols with the sequins; for example, a cross to represent redemption, a butterfly to represent new life, the chi rho to represent Christ, a triangle to represent the Trinity, a fish to represent a Christian.

The children should take the decorated candles home to use each night at dinnertime. Jesus is the light of the world. The candles remind us of Jesus' presence with us and call us to pray each night of the lenten season.

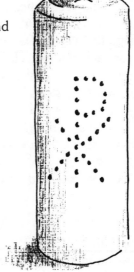

Scripture Chain

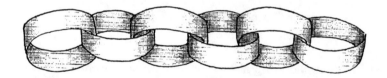

Christians need to become familiar with scripture. One way of learning what Jesus wants of us is to ponder his words and their meaning for our lives. A scripture chain provides an interesting way to do this with children.

This is a 40-link chain. Each day during Lent the child removes a link from the chain and reads the scripture verse inside. When the last link is removed, it is Easter. Links are not included for Sundays since these are not counted in the 40 days.

The bible verses include the text references in case the child—or parent—wants to look up the passage from which the verse is taken.

Type the words of Jesus and the references on masters and then copy them for each student. Have the children cut apart the bible verses. (For younger children, cut the verses apart and provide an envelope for each child with the 40 strips.) Pick any strip and form it into a loop with tape. Loop each successive link through the one before to form the chain. The loops can be added in any order.

Here are the bible verses:

You shall love the Lord your God
with your whole heart (Matthew 22:37).

I am the way, and the truth, and the life (John 14:6).

Ask, and you will receive (Matthew 7:7).

I am the good shepherd (John 10:11).

And know that I am with you always,
until the end of the world (Matthew 28:20).

The command I give you is this,
that you love one another (John 15:17).

Let the children come to me (Mark 10:14).

For the One whom God has sent
speaks the words of God (John 3:34).

Blest are they who show mercy; mercy shall be theirs (Matthew 5:7).

As the Father has loved me,
so I have loved you (John 15:9).

Come after me and I will make you fishers of men
(Matthew 4:19).

The gift you have received, give as a gift (Matthew 10:8).

What profit does he show who gains the whole world and destroys
himself in the process? (Luke 9:25).

If you seek perfection, go, sell your possessions, and give to the
poor (Matthew 19:21).

With God all things are possible (Mark 10:27).

Anyone who loves me
will be true to my word (John 14:23).

Go, therefore, and make disciples of all the nations (Matthew
28:19).

Do not let your hearts be troubled.
Have faith in God (John 14:1).

This is how all will know you for my disciples:
your love for one another (John 13:35).

Whoever believes in the Son
has life eternal (John 3:36).

Yes, God so loved the world
that he gave his only Son (John 3:16).

The harvest is good but the laborers are scarce (Matthew 9:37).

Love your enemy and do good (Luke 6:35).

I am the bread of life (John 6:48).

Little is forgiven the one whose love is small (Luke 7:47).

Your faith has been your salvation (Luke 7:50).

Do not be afraid! (Mark 6:50).

Your heavenly Father knows all that you need (Matthew 6:32).

Treat others the way you would have them treat you (Matthew
7:12).

Our Father in heaven,
hallowed be your name (Matthew 6:9).

Go into the whole world and proclaim the good news to all creation
(Mark 16:15).

Blest too the peacemakers; they shall be called sons of God (Matthew 5:9).

Live on in my love (John 15:9).

Be compassionate, as your father is compassionate (Luke 6:36).

He who is not with me is against me (Matthew 12:30).

Where two or three are gathered in my name, there am I in their midst (Matthew 18:20).

Many who are first shall come last, and the last shall be first (Mark 10:31).

Take this and eat it . . . this is my body (Matthew 26:26).

Follow me (Matthew 9:9).

I am the resurrection and the life (John 11:25).

Have the students take their scripture chains home. Hopefully, the scripture chain will be a source of inspiration to each child during the lenten season and beyond.

Pat-a-Pet Project

During Lent we should be especially concerned to follow Jesus' teachings to care about others. Children need to understand that caring means caring about people beyond their immediate families. A nursing home project is a good one for Lent because it enables the children to reach out to others. Many groups and organizations visit nursing homes at Christmas time, but people live in nursing homes the year around. The Pat-a-Pet Project is a heartwarming activity for Lent.

Many animal shelters are willing to participate in a project that brings animals to nursing homes. Make arrangements with the local animal shelter for this activity. It often works out well to schedule this project right after school because the animals usually have to be back at the animal shelter in time for the shift change.

Seek permission from the nursing home activity director for this project. Usually the animals should be removed before the evening meal is served.

The animal shelter will most often provide several small puppies and some kittens. The children take the animals around to visit the residents in the home. Children and animals make a wonderful combination. In a nursing home many residents do not get to see either very often.

Encourage the children to invite the residents to pet the animals. Caution the children that if people did like not like animals when they were younger, they won't like them any better when they are older.

If this activity works out well with the group, consider making it a monthly project. You may invite other classes to share in this activity.

Stations of the Cross Posters

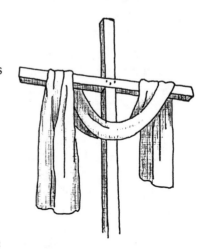

The traditional Way of the Cross commemorates Jesus' passion and death on Good Friday. We follow along in the footsteps of Jesus to remind us of the great love that Jesus has for us—even unto death. The Stations of the Cross remind us also that our crosses are very small in comparison

Many catechists now add a 15th station, the resurrection, to remind children that Jesus' death was not the end but the beginning of our life with him. His passion and death would have no meaning if he had not risen and conquered death for us. Encourage elementary students to reflect upon the Stations of the Cross by making a poster for each station. This is a good follow-up activity to a discussion of the Way of the Cross.

Provide each child in the class with a piece of white poster board. Have markers available to illustrate the stations. Before beginning, put the name of each station on a slip of paper. If you have more than 15 students, list some stations more than once. Place all the pieces of paper into a bowl. Let each student pick one at random. That will be the one that he or she illustrates. A large class can make more than one set of stations or children can work in pairs. Ask the children to use a black marker to put the number of the station and the description at the bottom of the poster board.

The Stations of the Cross are:

First station	Jesus is condemned
Second station	Jesus carries his cross
Third station	Jesus falls the first time
Fourth station	Jesus meets his mother
Fifth station	Simon helps Jesus carry his cross
Sixth station	Veronica wipes the face of Jesus
Seventh station	Jesus falls the second time
Eighth station	Jesus meets the women of Jerusalem
Ninth station	Jesus falls the third time
Tenth station	Jesus is stripped of his clothes

Eleventh station	Jesus is nailed to the cross
Twelfth station	Jesus dies on the cross
Thirteenth station	Jesus is taken down from the cross
Fourteenth station	Jesus is placed in the tomb
Fifteenth station	The resurrection of Jesus

When all the posters are completed, display them in the hallway. Use one wall, and place them in order. Not only are the posters a source of learning for the students who do them, but they provide something for the other students to think about as they walk down the hallway. They are a reminder that Jesus did indeed die for us and that he was raised from the dead.

Question Game

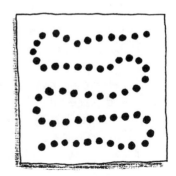

This board game is a fun way for children to recall facts about the Lent and Easter seasons. It can help them review information they already know and also help them learn new facts too.

The game board is made from a square of poster board. Fifty-eight self-adhesive circles, sold for marking file folders, form a path for tokens to follow. Mark 17 of the circles *Take a card*. The game starts in the lower left-hand corner on the first circle. It ends in the upper right-hand corner on the last circle. The game can be covered with clear self-adhesive plastic to make it last through repeated use.

Put lenten facts questions on index cards, one question and answer set on each card. To make duplicate sets of cards for several games, type one master list. Make duplicates on sheets of address labels (available from copier supply stores). Simply peel off the labels and place them on the index cards.

Here are some Lenten facts that can be used for this game:

Question: Who denied Jesus three times?
Answer: Peter.

Question: What day did Jesus die on the cross?
Answer: Good Friday.

Question: What is the time before Easter called?
Answer: Lent.

Question: Who said "Father forgive them, they do not know what they are doing"?
Answer: Jesus.

Question: Who betrayed Jesus?
Answer: Judas.

Question: What is the first day of Lent called?
Answer: Ash Wednesday.

Question: What symbol reminds us of Jesus' death?
Answer: The cross.

Question: On what road did the disciples see Jesus after his resurrection?
Answer: Road to Emmaus.

Question: On what day do we commemorate the Last Supper?
Answer: Holy Thursday.

Question: Who helped Jesus carry his cross?
Answer: Simon of Cyrene.

Question: How many days does Lent last?
Answer: 40

Question: What was the risen Jesus' first word to his apostles?
Answer: Peace.

Question: What type of crown did the soldiers put on Jesus' head.
Answer: Crown of thorns.

Question: Who was at the tomb when the women came early on Easter morning?
Answer: An angel.

Question: What Jewish feast was celebrated at the Last Supper?
Answer: Passover.

Question: Who handed Jesus over to be crucified?
Answer: Pilate.

Question: Where did Jesus go to pray on Holy Thursday night?
Answer: Garden of Gethsemane.

Question: On what day of each week do we remember Jesus' resurrection on Easter?
Answer: Sunday.

Question: Which apostle doubted that Jesus had risen?
Answer: Thomas.

Question: In what town did Jesus die?
Answer: Jerusalem.

Question: On which feast do we celebrate the resurrection of Jesus?
Answer: Easter.

Have the players take turns rolling a die and moving their tokens along the path. When the player lands on a take-a-card space, the person on the left asks the player the question on the top card. For a correct answer the player goes ahead one space. For an incorrect answer the player does not advance. Play continues until one or all players pass the finish space.

Prodigal Son

The parable of the Prodigal Son can be used during Lent to demonstrate to the children that our God is a loving and merciful God.

Read aloud this parable from Luke 15:11-32. Then discuss it with them. Ask questions to be sure they understood what happened in the story:

—How many sons did the father have?

—What did the younger son get from the father before he went away?

—After he spent all his money, what kind of job did the younger son get?

—What did he decide to do?

—Was this son sorry that he left home?

—Was his father happy to see him?

—Did the father love both his sons?

Explain to the children that Jesus told this story so that people would know that God loves us even when we do things that are wrong. God is like the father in the story. When we turn to him and tell him that we are sorry, he forgives us as the father in the story forgave his son. Tell the children that there is nothing for which God will not forgive us.

Ask the children to draw a picture of any part of the story that they wish. Tell them to label their papers *The Prodigal Son*. Drawing allows time for children to think about what they have heard. It helps them review the story in their minds and remember it.

Bible Spiral

Learning about God's word is important. During Lent we pause and reflect on how God reveals himself to us and how we are to live as Christians. To help students remember this idea during Lent, show them how to make a bible spiral with the following reminder from Luke 11:28 on it:

"Blest are they who hear the word of God and keep it."

Each child needs a sheet of construction paper of any color to make the spiral. First, tell the children to cut out a large circle. Then, beginning at the outside edge of the circle, they cut a one-inch strip around and around the inside until the middle is reached. You may want to draw the cut lines for younger children. Finally, have the students copy the verse clockwise around the spiral beginning in the middle.

When the lettering is finished, have the students thread a length of yarn through the middle to use for a hanger. When the paper is held up, the cut circle will become a spiral that twists around with the words of the Bible verse visible on it.

The spiral will be a reminder throughout Lent that we are to learn the word of God. We are to seek him in our lives. We are also to live his message in our lives as Christians during Lent and always.

Pretzel Legend

The story of the pretzel is an interesting one for children.

The legend claims that the pretzel was originated in the Middle Ages by monks. They formed dough into pretzels to look like arms folded in prayer. Then they gave the pretzels to children as a reward for learning their prayers.

Prayer is an important part of Lent. A class lenten project can be for the children to learn a new prayer.

After the morning prayer give each child a pretzel. Ask the students to look at the pretzels and see if they can see the arms folded in prayer. Explain that no one knows whether or not this legend is true, but that it is an interesting story. Encourage the children to pray in class and at home during Lent and always. Prayer should be woven into the fabric of our existence; it should be a part of everything we do.

Petition Prayer

Children learn to pray by praying. They need to learn to ask God's help for themselves and other people. It is part of our life as Christians to care about others. This means not only showing concern to other people, but praying for them as well. Our prayers are important.

Children can compose petition prayers that can be used as classroom prayers or at prayer service. When the teacher or group leader reads the petitions, the class responds "Lord, hear our prayer." Each group's petition prayer will be different because it will reflect the needs of the particular community. Here is an example of a petition prayer:

Leader: For people who go to bed hungry. . .

All: Lord, hear our prayer.

Leader: For all those who are ill. . .

All: Lord, hear our prayer.

Leader: For the homeless who have nowhere to go. . .

All: Lord, hear our prayer.

Leader: For those who are victims of poverty. . .

All: Lord, hear our prayer.

Leader: For lonely people everywhere. . .

All: Lord, hear our prayer.

Verse Flower

Lent is a time to grow in the love of God and in service to our neighbor. During Lent we should strive to care for others as Jesus told us to do. A verse flower will help the children remember Jesus' command: "Love your neighbor as yourself" (Matthew 22:39). The flower itself is a good symbol during Lent; as flowers grow toward the sun, we are to grow toward God.

Each child needs a sheet of blue construction paper for the background. Then help the children cut out a yellow center and five petals of any bright color for their flowers. They also need a green stem and two leaves.

Tell the children to write each word of the following verse on the petals: Love—your—neighbor—as—yourself. Have them print *Jesus said* on the yellow center. Then show them how to glue the petals around the center in order. Tell them to lay the petals on the paper correctly before gluing to be sure they have it right.

Talk to the children about what it means to love someone as much as yourself. Stress that this means a great deal of love. Ask them to name people who might be their neighbors in this phrase. Explain that neighbor does not mean just someone who lives by us; rather, it means everyone in God's family.

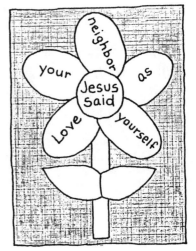

As followers of Jesus, we are to freely give of ourselves to others. This is not in hope of being repaid, but because God's love is freely given to us. This gift of love is meant to be passed on to others.

Encourage the children to display their flowers at home during Lent as a reminder that they are to grow in love during the Lent season.

Lenten Calendar

A lenten calendar gives children ideas for serving God in their lives. Each of the forty days of Lent offers a suggestion. Sundays are set aside for going to church.

Make a calendar for the days of Lent. Print an idea on the calendar for each day. Duplicate the calendar for the children to take home. Ideas for the calendar are:

Say the Our Father.

Pray for those who are ill.

Read Psalm 100.

Smile at someone today.

Tell someone thank you.

Forgive someone who hurt you.

Read Luke 17:11-19.

Share your time with someone.

Say a prayer at bedtime.

Stop and feel God's presence.

Say I'm sorry.

Find five signs of spring.

Read Mark 12:28-31.

Say a morning prayer.

Hug someone in your family.

Make a donation.

Thank God for three things.

Visit a neighbor.

Pray for peace.

Pray for those who are homeless.

Write a letter to someone.

Say thank you to God.

Read Luke 10:30-37.

Pray for those who are hungry.

Read Psalm 96.

Do a chore.

Help someone.

Take a walk and admire nature.
Talk to God about a problem.
Pray for those who are lonely.
Be kind to someone.
Pray for those who help us.
Compliment someone.
Help keep the world clean.
Cheer up someone who is sad.
Teach someone a new skill.
Pray for missionaries.
Make an Easter card.
Color eggs.
Read Matthew 28:1-10.

Encourage the children to do as many of these suggestions as they can during Lent. Most can be done without outside help. This calendar helps the children become aware of various ways that they can follow Jesus.

Prayer of St. Francis

The beautiful prayer of St. Francis gives expression to what it means to be a Christian. It is a meaningful prayer for Lent and captures what our Lent—and our lives—should be all about.

Read the prayer to the students at the beginning of class:

Lord, make me an instrument of your peace;
    where there is hatred, let me sow love;
    where there is injury, pardon;
    where there is doubt, faith;
    where there is despair, hope;
    where there is darkness, light;
    and where there is sadness, joy.

O Divine Master, grant that I may not so much seek
    to be consoled as to console,
    to be understood as to understand,
    to be loved as to love.

For it is in giving that we receive,
    it is in pardoning that we are pardoned,
    and it is in dying that we are born to eternal life.
    Amen.

Make a large copy of the prayer on poster board and place it on the bulletin board. Allow the children time to copy the prayer, or part of it, to take home.

This prayer has been recorded by several musical groups. If you have one of these recordings, play it for your class. Ask the children what they think this prayer means.

· 5 ·

The Hope of
EASTER

Easter is the most important feast of the church year. Jesus rose from the dead on that first Easter and forever changed the world.

Easter is a moveable feast. It is celebrated on the first Sunday after the first full moon of spring. Thus Easter is celebrated when the days are getting longer and signs of new life in nature are all around us. We rejoice in the new life that Jesus brings us. His resurrection gives us hope; we also will have new life after death because of Jesus. At Easter we reaffirm our belief in the resurrection.

Jesus' rising from the dead was proof indeed that he was the Son of God. His resurrection was God's sign of approval on all that Jesus did and taught. Jesus died a public death on the cross so that there would be no question that he did die and did live again. The cross thus became a sign of victory over death and a victory over sin.

Easter is not the end of the lenten season, but rather, the beginning for all of us. We are to put on the Lord, Jesus Christ. We need to bring this sense of beginnings, of celebration, of joy, of hope into our classrooms. We must encourage the children to celebrate Easter throughout their lives.

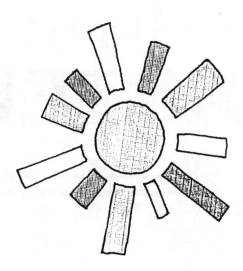

Newsletter

An Easter newsletter helps children find out how the parish celebrates the events of Holy Week and Easter. It makes these events more personal, not just something they read about in their books.

Students can work individually or in pairs to write stories for the newsletter. List possible topics for articles on the board and ask the children to choose the topics they want. Suggest ideas that involve interviews and also ones that can be researched. Some ideas are:

—Ask the pastor the times of the Holy Week services.

—Interview the Director of Religious Education about any special Holy Week or Easter projects.

—Ask some parents what special family activities they are planning for Easter Sunday.

—Interview several students about their favorite Easter custom.

—Research common Easter symbols such as palms, lilies, eggs and butterflies.

Give the students directions and hints; for example, remind them to contact the pastor or DRE and set up a time for the interview and suggest sources in the church library where they can find materials on Easter symbols. Some children may think of other story ideas. Give the students a deadline and ask them to provide a headline to go along with their stories.

When all the stories have been turned in, type them in a double-column style with the headlines in all capitals.

If possible, keep the newsletter to one page. More than that is time consuming to type and expensive to duplicate. Some stories may have to be shortened to fit this requirement. Of course, for a large class you will need more than one page.

Duplicate the newsletter for each student. They will have learned from their assignments, and they will learn more from reading what others have contributed.

Holy Week Panorama

During Holy Week we need to plan special activities for the children to help them learn about the significance of this special week in the church year. A panorama showing the events of Holy Week is a great idea for a hallway.

Begin by explaining that Holy Week is the week before Easter. Explain to the children that during this special week we recall important events in the final week of Jesus' life.

Holy Week begins with Palm Sunday, the day that Jesus entered Jerusalem for the last time. The people hailed him and put palm branches down on the road as he rode into town. That is why we receive palms at church on this day.

On Holy Thursday we commemorate the last meal that Jesus had with his apostles. This was the day that he gave us the Eucharist so that he would be always with us in a special way.

Then we come to Good Friday. It is a puzzle to many children why we call the day of Jesus' death on the cross a *good* day. Explain that if Jesus did not die, he could not have risen from the dead and brought new life to all of us.

Easter is the most important feast of the church year. On Easter we celebrate the hope that Jesus brought to all of us. The risen Christ continues to live among us. Easter is at the center of our faith as Christians. We are to live the new life of Easter in our daily lives. We are to attest to our belief in Easter by everything we say and do.

After a discussion about the meaning of Holy Week, divide the class into four groups. Assign each group one of the days of Holy Week that you have discussed. Ask the students to work together to make a poster depicting that day on a large sheet of white poster board. They can use markers for their illustration of the central event of that day.

The four posters are:

> Palm Sunday—the entry of Jesus into Jerusalem.
> Holy Thursday—Jesus at the Last Supper.
> Good Friday—Jesus on the cross.
> Easter—the empty tomb.

Ask each group to label the name of the day represented by their poster at the top. When the posters are finished, hang them in the hallway in chronological order. The posters are a learning experience for the students who make them, and also for those who see the posters displayed in the hallway during Holy Week.

Easter Cross

It is very important to help children connect the significance of the cross with the resurrection. Jesus' death has no meaning without his subsequent rising from the dead. The death of Jesus was not the end, but the beginning.

A simple craft project helps to visually express this concept to children. Pass out purple construction paper and show the children how to cut out crosses seven inches tall by five inches wide.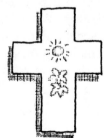

Provide new-life stickers—butterflies, flowers and other symbols—for each child. Have the children put one sticker on each end of the cross and one in the middle.

Christian bookstores also have Easter stickers showing Jesus coming from the tomb and talking to his followers after his resurrection.

These Easter crosses help the children understand that the resurrection of Jesus is the fulfillment of the cross.

This is a simple, easy-to-do project that appeals especially to younger children and does not require lengthy preparation or expensive materials. Yet these crosses are visual reminders of the meaning of Christ's death and resurrection.

Easter Echo Pantomime

An echo pantomime retells a bible story using short phrases and actions. The teacher says the first phrase in the story and does the accompanying motion. Then the children repeat—echo—the words and motion. Pantomimes actively involve the children in the telling of the story.

This is the story of the first Easter:[1]

Early on Easter morning	(stretch)
friends of Jesus went to his tomb.	(walk in place)
They found the big stone	(point)
rolled back from the entrance.	(pretend to push)
They looked at one another	(look at others)
because they were amazed.	(shrug shoulders)
They went into the tomb	(walk in place)
and looked for Jesus.	(look from side to side)
They couldn't find him.	(shake head no)
An angel came	(arms outstretched)
and told them Jesus had risen.	(hands cup mouth)
They ran out of the tomb	(run in place)
and told Peter what had happened.	(point in the distance)
Peter ran to the tomb	(run in place)
and looked inside.	(look from side to side)
It was empty.	(shake head yes)
Later Jesus appeared	(arms outstretched)
and told people the good news.	(hands cup mouth)

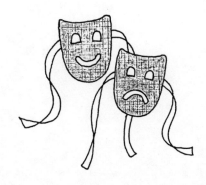

Easter Lily

The Easter lily has long been used as a symbol of Easter. The pure white lily represents the risen Christ. Some have likened the root from which it grows to a tomb.

Bring an Easter lily to class, if possible. Explain the lily as a symbol of Jesus to the children. Leave the lily in the classroom after Easter as a reminder of the risen Christ.

When the children see the church decorated with Easter lilies, they will be reminded of the true meaning of Easter.

Have the children draw a picture of an Easter lily using the one in the classroom as a model. They can take home their pictures to remind them of Jesus at Easter.

Butterfly Mosaic

Even young children can make lovely butterfly mosaics which serve as reminders of the meaning of the Easter season. The butterfly symbolizes resurrection. As Christ was laid in a dark tomb, then rose to even greater glory, so the caterpillar emerges from his cocoon after undergoing a startling transformation.

Each child needs a sheet of construction paper on which to make the butterfly. Provide a cardboard pattern of a large butterfly so the children can trace the outline. (Provide paper with the outline already done for very young children.) Each background sheet should also bear the words *Easter brings new life*.

Cut brightly colored construction paper into three-quarter-inch squares. Have the children glue these paper squares onto the wings of their butterflies in whatever arrangement suits them. This is a good project for children because they have the freedom to do it their way.

This simple, inexpensive art idea produces bright, beautiful butterflies that are individual to each child. This project helps children express their Easter joy.

Hang the butterflies in the hallway as a celebration of Easter and Jesus' resurrection.

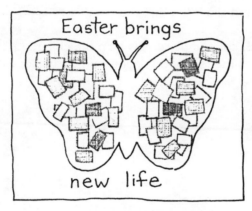

Easter Placemats

Easter is a time when we Christians should be so full of joy that we naturally want to share it with others. Easter placemats are an inexpensive way of brightening the day for people in nursing homes who will eat their Easter dinner from trays.

Check with the activity director of a local nursing home for approval before beginning this project. Also find out how many placemats are needed and arrange a delivery date and time.

Make the placemats from wallpaper sample books. Many stores are happy to give away books of discontinued patterns. Before class, cut the sheets out of the book. Choose bright, cheerful patterns in Easter colors. Also provide an assortment of paper napkins in complementary colors.

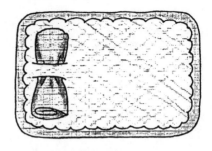

Allow each child to choose a wallpaper sample. Have them scallop the edge, fringe it, or otherwise trim it to their satisfaction. Be sure that they do not cut away too much! Then, on the left-hand side of each placemat, have the children cut two horizontal slits about an inch apart. Have each child pick a color-coordinated napkin, fold it attractively, and slip it through the slit.

These cheerful, colorful placemats help the children put their good intentions to work as they share the joyful spirit of Easter with the residents of the nursing home.

Coded Message

Children enjoy the challenge of deciphering secret codes. Using coded messages can help them learn and remember what the Easter season is all about.

For each child, draw a large egg shape on a piece of paper. Within the egg outline put as many small lines as there are letters in the message. Leave a blank space between words. Here are some sample Easter messages:

—Jesus brings new life.

—Jesus has risen. Alleluia.

—Easter brings hope to all.

Under each line in the message put the number that corresponds to the correct letter in the code. The secret code follows:

a = 1, b = 2, c = 3, d = 4, e = 5, f = 6, g = 7, h = 8, i = 9, j = 10, k = 11, l = 12, m = 13, n = 14, o = 15, p = 16, q = 17, r = 18, s = 19, t = 20, u = 21, v = 22, w = 23, x = 24, y = 25, z = 26.

There is something about mysteries and secret codes that children enjoy. This type of activity will help them remember the point of the lesson.

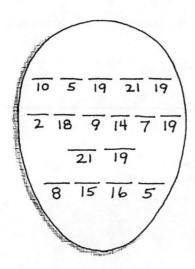

Easter Prayer

Prayer is an important part of the Easter season. It is one of the ways in which we respond to the Easter experience of new life through Jesus. Prayer helps us express the feelings of joy and hope that Easter brings.

Dear God,
We thank you for sending Jesus to us.
We praise you for the new life of Easter.
All around us we see signs of new life—
flowers blooming,
birds singing,
children laughing.
Help us to see your presence in springtime.
We have new life because Jesus rose on Easter.
Help us to be an Easter people.
Help us to learn to love others as you love us.
Help us to share the good news of Easter with others.
May the joy and hope of the Easter season fill our
lives now and always.
We ask this in the name of our Lord Jesus Christ. Amen.

This prayer of praise and petition can be used as a class prayer during the Easter season. Or you can write your own Easter prayer.

Alleluia Banner

An alleluia banner is a good way for children to share some of their Easter joy with others. A banner also shows the children what they can do when they work together.

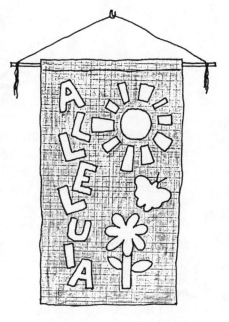

Use a neutral shade of burlap for the background of the alleluia banner. If you plan to display the banner in the vestibule, make it nine feet long by four feet wide. For the classroom, four feet long by three feet wide is sufficient. The procedure for either size banner is the same.

Make the decorations for the banner from brightly colored felt. Use symbols of the new life of Easter such as a yellow sun, a purple cross, an orange butterfly, a red flower with green stem and leaves. Cut the theme word, *Alleluia*, from green felt. This word summarizes the Easter experience. Provide patterns that the children can use to cut out the letters and symbols for the banner.

Spread newspapers on the floor and put the burlap backing on top. Glue the letters and symbols onto the burlap. The letters spelling *Alleluia* can be placed vertically down the left side of the banner and the new-life symbols on the right side. This part of the project requires careful supervision.

The alleluia banner helps children visually express the hope of Easter time. It can be hung year after year to proclaim the good news to all who see it.

New-Life Walk

We can introduce young children to the concept of the resurrection by helping them become aware of the new life around them. Spring reminds them, and us, of the new life that Jesus brings to us by his resurrection.

Learning by doing is important with young children. They need to actively participate in the learning process if they are to understand and remember what we try to teach them. For this reason, a new-life walk is an excellent way to help children learn about Easter.

Take the children outside the classroom and walk with them around the grounds. Point out signs of new life—grass growing, buds on trees, bird nests, flowers blooming. Allow plenty of time for them to look as you show them these things. Encourage them to point out additional signs of new life.

In the classroom, review some of the things that the children saw on the walk. Explain that Jesus brings us new life at Easter because he was raised from the dead on the first Easter. The signs of new life all around us remind us of the new life of Easter.

Praise-God Mural

A praise-God mural features pictures of the new life at Easter time. It allows the children to praise God for sending us Jesus and for the signs of new life that are all around us in the spring.

Provide a long sheet of butcher paper. In large block letters spell out *Praise God*. Provide pictures of new life that the children can glue inside the outline of the letters. Garden catalogs are a good source of all kinds of spring plants and flowers. These catalogs are available upon request from mail order garden suppliers.

Let each child choose pictures and glue them onto the mural. When completed, the bright, colorful pictures will spell out the letters in *Praise God*.

The mural ties together the idea of new life with God. It also helps the children learn to work together and shows them what can be accomplished when they do. Use the mural as a bulletin-board decoration for the time after Easter. It is a colorful reminder to praise God for sending us his Son at Easter.

Choral Reading

An Easter choral reading can help children express the spirit of joy and hope of the season. The activity involves all the children in the class. The children can read their parts so no memorization is necessary.

A choral reading is a good presentation for an older class to do for a younger class. It can also be used as part of an Easter prayer service or liturgy.

Let Bells Ring[2]

Chorus: Let bells ring with joy—
The Savior lives!
Let bells ring with joy—
The Savior lives!

Solo 1: He who died has risen!

Solo 2: Risen to show us the way,

Solo 3: Risen on a wonderful morning,

Solo 4: Risen on Easter day!

Chorus: Let bells ring with joy—
The Savior lives!
Let bells ring with joy—
The Savior lives!

Solo 5: Joy to the world this Easter!

Chorus: He lives, he lives, he lives!
When we forget to follow,

Solo 6: Jesus forgives, he forgives!

Chorus: Let bells ring with joy—
The Savior lives!
Let bells ring with joy—
The Savior lives!

Solo 7: All birds of the air fly higher;

Solo 8: All beautiful flowers bloom.

Solo 9: This is the glory of Easter!

Solo 10: Everywhere people shout!

Chorus: Let bells ring with joy—
The Savior lives!
Let bells ring with joy—
The Savior lives!

A choral reading helps children share the good news of the Easter season with others and involves them as part of the Easter celebration.

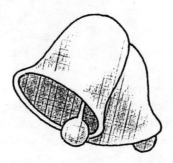

Easter Chick

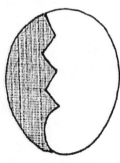

Fig. 1   Fig. 2

New-life symbols help young children understand the feast of Easter. They relate the new life of spring to the new life Jesus brings at Easter.

A good new-life symbol to use with young children is a chick hatching from an egg. Eggs are a symbol long associated with the new life of Easter.

Help each child make a chick that hatches from a paper egg.

Have each child cut a yellow chick from construction paper. (Draw the outline of the chick on the paper before class.) A black dot from a marker makes the eye for the chick.

Then have each child make an egg for the chick out of green construction paper which is folded in half. You will need to draw lines for younger children to cut along. First, have the children cut an egg shape through both thicknesses of paper. Then, keeping the two pieces together, have them cut a jagged edge. Discard the smaller piece of each egg, shown by the unshaded portion in Figure 1. Warn them that they should not cut all the way to the center of the shape. Some children may need help with this.

To assemble the Easter chick and egg, use a brad pushed through both egg halves and the bottom of the chick. The children will be able to pull the egg apart and see the chick hatch over and over. As a final touch, have the children decorate their eggs with Easter chick stickers.

Doorknob Sign

Doorknob signs help children make the connection between springtime and the new life Jesus brings us as Christians. These signs proclaim the good news of Easter.

Have the children each cut out a rectangle, nine inches by four-and-a-half inches, from brightly colored construction paper. About an inch down from the top tell them to cut out a circle so that the signs can be hung over a doorknob.

In the middle of each sign have the children print *Jesus brings new life*. Then let the children choose new-life stickers to decorate their signs. Stickers of butterflies, flowers, birds, the sun, green leaves and others can be found in most greeting-card stores.

Younger children can also complete this project if the signs are cut out for them and lettered before class. Then the children can choose the stickers they want to use to decorate the signs.

These doorknob signs share the joyful message of Easter with all who pass by. The stickers are colorful and help the children associate Easter and new life. The children can take their doorknob signs home to display as a reminder of the Easter message.

Praise Litany

Prayer should be seasonal; it should reflect what is going on in our lives. During the Easter season children should praise the Lord for new life. A praise litany is a good activity for even very young children.

Older children can help compose their own prayer. As the children suggest signs of new life, the teacher can print them on the board. The words become a litany when the children respond, "We praise you, Lord," after the teacher says each phrase.

Easter Prayer

Teacher: For warm sunshine . . .

Children: We praise you, Lord.

Teacher: For yellow daffodils . . .

Children: We praise you, Lord.

Teacher: For new leaves on trees . . .

Children: We praise you, Lord.

Teacher: For beautiful butterflies . . .

Children: We praise you, Lord.

Teacher: For green grass . . .

Children: We praise you, Lord.

Teacher: For all new life at Easter . . .

Children: We praise you, Lord.

Children like this kind of prayer because they can relate the images to their own lives.

Easter Haiku

The haiku is a Japanese poetry form. It is especially suited to the Easter season because it centers on nature. The new life of the Easter season provides many visual pictures that can be expressed in this type of poetry. The haiku attempts to capture a moment in time. It brings to life a part of the Easter season through words that convey images.

The haiku is a three-line poem. It consists of 17 syllables, five in the first and last lines, and seven in the middle line. Have the class work together to compose a haiku which the teacher writes on the blackboard before asking the children to compose their own poems.

The following is a haiku about tulips:

> Spring brings bright tulips
> Pushing from below the ground
> Reaching for the sun.

The lines of a haiku do not rhyme. Haiku is a good type of poetry to use with children because it has form to help them but also allows freedom of expression. Writing haiku poetry is a good follow-up activity to a discussion of the new life we see all around us at Easter.

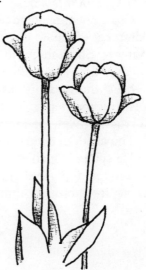

Easter-Symbol Triptych

We can help the children understand abstract concepts by relating them to something they already know. Spring symbols can be used to explain the new life that Jesus brought us on the first Easter.

Talk with the class about symbols which have come to be associated with Easter: butterflies, eggs, bunnies, birds, chicks, flowers. Explain that the cross is an Easter symbol because Jesus had to die before he could come back to life. The connection between Jesus' death and the new life of Easter is a very important one for the children. It can be demonstrated by an Easter-symbol triptych.

Use a sheet of standard construction paper for each triptych. Have the children cut off about one inch from the long side and then fold the paper into thirds. Show them how to scallop the top edges by cutting the two sides in a curve down from the middle.

Have the students cut crosses and new-life symbols from bright colors of construction paper. Each child will need two new-life symbols in addition to a cross. Provide patterns for those who cannot draw freehand.

The children should glue the cross in the middle section. Then glue new-life symbols such as a butterfly and a flower on the sides. This makes a free-standing triptych that can be displayed at home as a reminder of the new life Jesus brought through his death and resurrection.

Bible Verse Stand-up

"I am the resurrection and the life" sums up the experience of Jesus' resurrection. This is a wonderful verse to remember and think about. A good way to help children remember this bible verse is to make bible verse stand-ups to take home.

Provide brightly colored sheets of construction paper. Each child will need a quarter of a sheet. Show them how to fold their papers in half to make a stand-up.

On the front of each stand-up, have the children print the bible verse. Add the reference, John 11:25, underneath with a fine-line marker.

Provide new-life stickers for the children. Christian bookstores often have Easter stickers showing Jesus after his resurrection. Tell the children to put a sticker on the left side of the stand-up next to the Bible verse.

The children can display their stand-ups at home as a reminder that we have life through Jesus Christ.

Butterfly Suncatcher

The butterfly is a good symbol of the resurrection. Its emergence from the cocoon reminds us of the rising of Jesus from the dead on Easter Sunday.

Children can make colorful butterfly suncatchers to take home and hang in their window to remind them of Easter. To make suncatchers, use construction paper and colorful sheets of tissue paper. Green, blue, yellow, purple and other bright colors of tissue paper are available at craft stores. The tissue paper is thin enough to let the sun shine through it.

Allow the children to pick out coordinating colors of construction paper and tissue paper. From half a sheet of construction paper have them cut out a butterfly shape. Provide a pattern that they can use for this. Next, show them how to cut around the inside of the butterfly outline leaving only a half-inch frame around the wings.

Have the children put glue around the butterfly shape and then lay it on the tissue paper. They should carefully cut away the excess tissue so that it does not extend beyond the outside edge of the butterfly. As a finishing touch, the children can cut out construction paper circles and glue them onto the tissue wings.

A piece of double-stick tape on the back of the butterfly's body will allow it to be placed in a window at home. The light comes through the tissue wings and creates a lovely effect. The butterfly suncatcher speaks of the glory of the Easter season without words.

Word Bingo

The Easter season has a special vocabulary all its own. Children need to become familiar with words that are used during this time of the church year. Easter word bingo helps them to do this. The game is played like regular bingo, but words are used instead of numbers.

To make an Easter bingo game, cut two-and-a-half inches from the bottom of a piece of standard typing paper. This makes a piece that is eight-and-a-half inches square. Use a pen and ruler to draw lines dividing each page into sixteen equal squares. Duplicate this page.

On each square of each page, print or type a word associated with the Easter season. Each card needs a slightly different arrangement of words so that all the children will not have bingo at the same time.

The following words are drawn from the gospels and church liturgy:

Angel	Lent
Barabbas	Life
Cross	Love
Easter	Mary
Emmaus	Mary Magdalene
Faith	Palm Sunday
Father	Passover
Forgiveness	Peace
Gethsemane	Peter
Glory	Pilate
Good Friday	Redemption
Holy Spirit	Resurrection
Holy Thursday	Sanhedrin
Jerusalem	Sin
Jesus	Temple
John	Thomas
Joy	Thorns
Judas	Tomb
Last Supper	Vigil

Easter	Thorns	Life	Sin
Glory	Jesus	Lent	Joy
Faith	Peter	Tomb	Thomas
John	Cross	Father	Peace

Make a bingo master—a sheet with all the words on it. Duplicate the master and cut it into squares. These are the caller's cards. Put them in a box and mix them up. The caller then picks a word at random and calls it out. To keep track of what has been called, the caller places the word over the same word on the master sheet.

The children who have the word that is called on the bingo card in front of them put a marker over it. The markers can be small squares of brightly colored poster board. Play continues until one child has four covered squares in a row. That child calls out bingo. The covered squares should be checked against the caller's sheet. Small holy cards or bible bookmarks make good prizes.

This game is a good follow-up to a unit on Easter because it helps children remember the words that they have learned. It is an interesting and entertaining way to review vocabulary.

New-Life Mural

Children can learn about the new life of the Easter season by making a three-dimensional new-life mural. This is a good way to involve all the children in learning by doing.

Use a length of butcher paper for the background. Lay it flat on a long table or the floor. Have the children cut out new-life symbols and glue them onto the paper to make the mural. The children should work under the supervision of the teacher regarding placement of the various items on the paper. Allow the children to be as creative as possible.

A bright yellow sun and a brown tree trunk with bare branches can be cut out of construction paper. Long strips of green construction paper that is fringed along one side with scissors form grass. Cut leaves from green self-adhesive paper to make the tree come alive.

Flowers with green paper stems and leaves "bloom" by gluing paper candy cups to the top of the stem.

Add colorful, three-dimensional butterflies. Ask the children to cut out butterfly shapes. Then show them how to fold both wings forward where they join the body and glue the body onto the mural.

Have a child who prints well write *Jesus Brings New Life* on the mural with a bright blue marker.

Allow the mural to dry, then hang it in the hallway for all to admire. The mural will proclaim the joy of the Easter season to all who pass by it.

·6·

The Spirit of

PENTECOST

The Easter season is not complete until Pentecost which we celebrate 50 days after Easter Sunday. On Pentecost Jesus fulfilled his promise to send the Holy Spirit.

The presence of the Holy Spirit gave the apostles strength to accomplish what they could never have done on their own. Filled with the Spirit, Peter, the man who had denied Jesus three times, led the early Christian church. Christianity spread near and far as the Spirit-filled apostles preached the good news.

Pentecost is celebrated as the birthday of the church. This feast reminds us that although we are different nations and different cultures, we are united in faith. We worship the God who made us all. We are a people of hope who do not fear the differences among us but see them as enriching the church.

The Holy Spirit lives in the church and in each one of us. The message of Pentecost is that we too are to be open to the Spirit in our lives. The church does not exist for itself, but through the Holy Spirit the church points the way to Christ. The church exists for all people. It is not tied to a particular time, place, culture or class. Through the church the good news of Christ's love is made known to all.

We are to open our minds and our hearts to the Holy Spirit at work in our lives. We are to say yes to God's call in our lives. We must respond with a total commitment. Christianity is a way of life. We must be a people of hope who believe in Jesus Christ and are committed to serving others. We must witness with our lives to his teachings. Christianity is not something that is added to our lives; it is who we were created to be from the beginning.

Christianity should shape our lives and everything that we do. We are to use our God-given gifts for the good of others and to glorify God as his creation. We must show God our gratitude for his love by sharing that love with others.

The gift of faith is not complete until it is shared. This is what it means to live as a Christian. We were created to live in community with others. We need other people, and they need us. We must share the love of God freely with other people as it was freely shared with us by Jesus Christ.

We are called to live as witnesses to Jesus Christ. Each of us is to proclaim the good new that Jesus brought. Pentecost reminds us that through the presence of the Holy Spirit in our lives, we are to continue the ministry of Jesus Christ, who came not to be served, but to serve.

Story of Pentecost

Read the story of Pentecost to the students from the Bible. It is found in Acts 2:1-11. Ask the children questions to help them understand what this story means.

— What feast day is this Bible passage about? (Pentecost)

— Who came to the followers of Jesus on that day? (Holy Spirit)

— What does the wind symbolize? (power and change)

— Who had promised to send the Holy Spirit? (Jesus)

— Why did the Holy Spirit appear as fire? (visible symbol of God's presence from the Old Testament)

— What did the apostles do after the Holy Spirit came? (preached to the people in Jerusalem)

— What was the purpose of the gift of languages? (to show that Jesus came for people of all nations)

— What change occurred in the apostles? (from frightened men in hiding to fearless public witnesses for Christ)

— How does the Holy Spirit help us? (lives in each one of us to guide us in all we do)

Encourage the students to ask questions of their own and to contribute their ideas to this discussion.

Pentecost Verse

Pentecost is a very important feast. It is celebrated as the birthday of the church. Remind the children that it is through the church that we witness to Christ in our lives and make him visible to other people. The Holy Spirit guides the church so that the faith is handed on from generation to generation.

As a reminder of what happened on Pentecost, show each child how to make a Pentecost verse to take home. Have the children cut a large tongue of fire from red paper. Remind the children that the Holy Spirit came in this way. Also point out that red is the symbolic color for Pentecost because it is the color of fire.

Have the children glue the tongue of fire to a sheet of white construction paper. On the top of the sheet, tell them to print the word *Pentecost.* On the red flame they should print the words: "All were filled with the Holy Spirit." Ask them to put the reference, "Acts 2:4," at the bottom of the paper.

This project is a visible reminder to the children of what we celebrate on Pentecost.

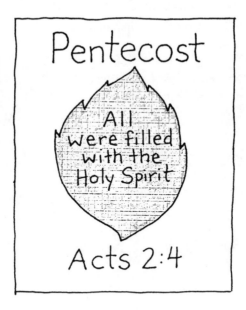

Gifts of the Spirit

We are each called to witness to the gospel in our own way. We are each called to a life with God. Each of us has unique talents and gifts to share with others.

In 1 Corinthians 12:4-7 Paul expresses well the idea of gifts of the Holy Spirit: "There are different gifts but the same Spirit; there are different ministries but the same Lord; there are different works but the same God who accomplishes all of them in everyone. To each person the manifestation of the Spirit is given for the common good."

We are not given gifts to use for ourselves, but for others. We have been created with unique talents and abilities that we can use for the good of all God's people.

As we discuss these verses with the students, we must stress that each of us is given a gift to use for others. This gift is meant to be shared. Have them think about what their gifts might be. See if they can name people they know or have heard about who are using their gifts for others.

Ask the children to think about how they might use their gifts in the future. Ask them to draw a picture of what they might be doing as adults to minister to others. Some may become teachers or doctors; others will work in nursing homes or state schools. Some will volunteer their time and talents to a special group; others may become foster parents. There are many possibilities for service.

This drawing project helps the students think about serving God in the future. It provides the opportunity for them to consider their individual gifts and how they might best use them. They may think about career choices that they had never previously considered. Most important, it reminds them that each of us is called to serve.

Christian Acrostic

At Pentecost the followers of Jesus received the Spirit. They went out to preach and to teach others the way of Jesus. The followers of Christ became known as Christians. We must help the children focus on what it means to be a Christian, to be a person who follows Christ. Students need the opportunity to synthesize all that they hear about in class and apply it to their lives.

One way to encourage students to think about being Christian is to ask them to make an acrostic from the word *Christian*. The acrostic form uses each letter in the key word to begin a word or phrase about the theme. When doing an acrostic about being a Christian, it is best to use phrases for each letter.

An acrostic using the word *Christian* turns out to be a summary of what the word means in our lives. Such an acrostic turns out like this:

Concerned about others

Helps those in need

Reads the word of God

Interested in others

Says prayers

Tells the good news of Jesus

Identified by love

Adores God

Needs others

It is helpful to do a sample acrostic with the children on the bulletin board to show them how it is done. Then encourage each individual to make a personal acrostic using the word *Christian* as the theme.

Good News Chain

When Jesus appeared to the apostles after his resurrection, he told them to tell others the good news. To help children remember this message of Jesus, show them how to make a paper chain that links together the words of Mark 16:15: "Proclaim the good news to all creation."

Duplicate the words on brightly colored paper. Each word should be on a different color. Use a paper cutter to cut the paper so that each word is on a strip of paper about one-inch wide. Put each word in a different box and arrange the boxes in the order of the verse; for example, the first box would have in it all the strips labeled *Proclaim*.

Let the children assemble paper chains that spell out the words in order. Tape works better than glue because it sticks right away. Show the children how to link one strip through another. When they finish, they will each have a brightly colored chain. Working on the chain will help them learn this bible verse.

Explain to the children that telling others the good news about Jesus is the joyous task of all the church. Discuss ways that they and others can tell the good news.

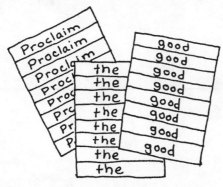

Missionaries

Missionaries help to spread the word of God to others. Being a missionary is the way some people answer God's call in their lives.

Place information about various missionary projects on a bulletin board in the hallway to help students become aware of the work of missionaries. Use pictures and captions of missionaries at work to make an attractive bulletin board display for the classroom. Back each picture with colored construction paper cut larger than the picture to form a frame. (Many missionary orders publish magazines with information about their activities. These are available by writing to the order. Addresses can be found in many religious magazines.)

Tell the children about some of the projects in which missionaries are involved, for example, spreading the word of God, health care, agriculture, education. Be sure to point out that we should support the missionary work by our offerings and our prayers.

Handprint Altar Cloth

An altar cloth featuring the handprints of the children is an especially effective project during the time of Pentecost. Our hands are symbols of ourselves. By using handprints on an altar cloth we show the children that they are important members of God's family. Our handprints are also unique and symbolize the unique talents that we each have to give to Christ.

Use a large white cloth that has been cut and hemmed to fit the altar. Mix bright colors of powdered tempera in aluminum pie pans for the handprints. The pie pans will not tip, and the paint can be mixed thick to give good results. Have a small bucket with soapy water nearby and a towel for cleanup.

With supervision, have each child dip a hand into the paint and press that hand firmly upon the cloth which has been laid out on a table. Show the children where to place their handprints for a uniform result. The handprints should not be too close together. Each hand should then go directly into the soapy water. Print each child's name by his or her handprint.

Let the cloth dry thoroughly before moving it. It can be used as an altar cloth for community worship or on a smaller altar used for prayer services by the children.

Pentecost Echo Pantomime

An excellent way to directly involve the children in the telling of a bible story is to use an echo pantomime. The teacher says a line and does the accompanying action. Then the children echo the words and action.

Story of Pentecost[1]

When the day of Pentecost came, the disciples were together.	(start with arms stretched out, and then move them in toward shoulder)
Suddenly,	(jump back)
there was a noise from the sky blowing.	(sway from side to side)
It filled the whole house.	(hands at sides, move upward)
Then they saw	(put hands over eyes)
what looked like tongues of fire	(palms together, move arms)
that touched each person there.	(pretend to touch people's heads)
They were filled with the Holy Spirit	(start at shoulders, and move hands down sides of body)
and began to talk in other languages.	(put hand to mouth, and move out)
The people outside heard them	(cup ear)
and gathered around.	(motion with arm to join)
They were surprised to hear	(cup ear)
their own languages spoken by the disciples.	(point to self)
It was so strange!	(palms up, extend arms out)
"Are those friends of Jesus?"	(point right finger)
"What is the matter with them?"	(point left finger)
Then Peter stood up to say,	(stand up straight, arms at sides)
"We are happy	(smile)
because God has kept a promise."	(point up to sky)
Peter talked to the people	(move right hand to mouth and out)
and told them the good news	(move left hand to mouth and out)
that God	(point up to the sky)

had raised Jesus from the dead. (rising movement with hands)
Many people believed Peter. (move right hand from self out)
The Spirit was with them. (move hands down body)
That happened long, long ago, (push hand outward)
but it is still like that today (shake finger)
because God (point up to sky)
made the promise to everyone, (make sweeping movement with arms)

even to us. (point to self)

Children enjoy acting out a story in this manner. It is easy to do line by line and there is no reading involved. This echo pantomime for Pentecost helps the children remember what the feast is all about.

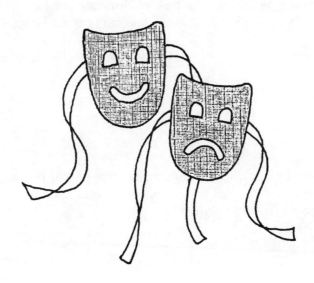

Pentecost Poetry

Poetry helps students consider the meaning of Pentecost. Poetry with a specific form is easiest for children to do. Such a poetic form is the cinquain, a five-line poem. Follow this format:

Line 1:   one-word title
Line 2:   two descriptive words
Line 3:   three action words
Line 4:   four words about the title
Line 5:   one-word synonym for the title

Let the students choose the subject of the poem and write individual cinquains. Good topics during the time of Pentecost are Pentecost, church, community and people. The following cinquain is about people[2]:

People

concerned, loving

praying, helping, forgiving

share God's peace together

community

This poetry form allows the children to write poems that speak to them about their own lives. It helps them understand and remember what Pentecost and being a Christian mean.

Word Guess

P _ n t _ c _ s t

This game helps children become familiar with words associated with Pentecost and the early church.

This game is played by two teams. Have the class count off by twos. All the ones form one team and all the twos form the other. The teams take turns guessing letters in a word represented on the chalkboard by lines. Each line equals one letter in the mystery word.

Use words associated with Pentecost and church. Put the lines on the board for the first word and invite one child from each team to come forward while the rest remain seated. The two students take turns guessing a letter that is in the word. If a correct letter is guessed, the teacher fills it in above the line representing that letter. Then the player goes again. If an incorrect guess is made, the play passes to the other player. The game continues until one of the players correctly guesses the word. That player's team gets one point and two more players come forward.

Players continue to come forward two at a time until all the players have had a turn. A player on one team can play twice if the teams are uneven. The team guessing the most words wins.

Some suggested words for this game are:

Peter	church
disciples	Jesus
community	faith
witness	love
Spirit	Paul
Pentecost	Christian

Peace Spiral

When Jesus appeared to his disciples after his resurrection, he said, "Peace be with you" (Jn 20:26). It is this peace that we are to seek in our world with the help of the Holy Spirit.

As people who follow Jesus we must be committed to peace. We must strive to bring his peace to others.

Talk to the children about ways that we can promote peace in our families and in our world. Encourage them to think of creative ways to solve problems. Ask them to bring to class magazine or newspaper accounts about people who work for peace. As reminders that we are all to promote peace, show them how to make peace spirals.

Provide one sheet of 9″ x 12″ red paper and half a sheet of white paper for each child. For younger children furnish sheets with cutting lines already duplicated. To make spirals, have the children cut the red sheet into a one-inch ribbon beginning at the outside of the paper and cutting in a circle toward the middle. Thread a string through one end and hang it so the paper forms a long spiral.

Next, have the students cut out block letters from the white paper spelling *peace*. Show them how to link the letters together with string and hang them down through the center of the spiral. The children can hang up their peace spirals at home to remind them that Christians are to be people of peace.

Burlap Banner

Proclaim to all that the Holy Spirit is present among us by making a Pentecost banner. Display the banner in the church vestibule or in the classroom as a sign of the Holy Spirit.

Ask an artistic person to design the banner and make paper patterns for symbols. Burlap can be used for the background. A wooden dowel threaded through a rod pocket at the top will make the banner easy to hang. Use felt for the words and symbols on the banner.

The students can cut out the felt pieces using the patterns. A dove and a flame are good symbols for Pentecost. Also have some wording on the banner. Felt letters can spell out *Pentecost* or *Come, Holy Spirit*. Craft glue works well and won't show through. Be sure to put paper underneath the banner so that the glue doesn't get on the floor or carpeting. Ask the students to follow the diagram for placement of the symbols and letters so that there is room for everything.

A banner has lasting value. It can be hung each year to announce the presence of the Holy Spirit.

Pentecost Play

A play allows children to act out the events of Pentecost and enables them to understand and remember what went on that day. The following Pentecost play is an excellent one for children.[3] It is a good one for an older grade to present to a younger one.

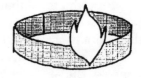

CAST: Narrator, Disciples, Mary, John, Peter, Man From Crowd, Woman From Crowd, Crowd.

PROPS: Head bands with flames pasted on. Stool on which Peter can stand.

SCENE ONE: Inside the Upper Room

NARRATOR: After Jesus went back to heaven, his friends got together to pray. They asked God to show them how to tell all the people in the world about Jesus. Mary, the Mother of Jesus, was with them.

MARY: I really miss Jesus. We're all going to miss him very much.

JOHN: Well, Mary, he said he would be with us forever, so I guess he's here with us right now, only in a different way.

MARY: I know, John. But I miss seeing him.

NARRATOR: All of a sudden without any warning a loud noise filled the room. It sounded like the noise the wind makes when it's blowing hard. The friends of Jesus saw little flames of fire spreading out all over the room. The flames settled on each one's head. At first they were scared but they realized it must be the Holy Spirit—sent by Jesus to be with them always.

DISCIPLES: What's happening? It's a sign from Jesus!

JOHN: This is the sign that the Spirit promised by Jesus is here with us right now. What a great day!

MARY: All the people must know about this.

DISCIPLES: Yes, Mary's right. Peter, go out and shout the good news.

SCENE TWO: Outside on the balcony

PETER: Listen to me, everyone. A great thing just happened. The Spirit of God has been sent to us.

MAN FROM CROWD: What's going on? What is he shouting about?

WOMAN FROM CROWD: Be quiet. Let's listen to the man.

PETER: Jesus was God's Son, and he did all kinds of great things. He cured the sick. He raised the dead. He preached the message of love and forgiveness. But he scared the powerful with his message. So they killed him.

But I have good news. God raised Jesus to life again. We all saw him. He went back to heaven, but today has sent his Spirit to us.

MAN FROM CROWD: But what about us?

PETER: You can all be baptized and believe in Jesus. Come now and receive God's gift—the Holy Spirit.

WOMAN FROM CROWD: Today is the day the Lord has made. Let us rejoice.

NARRATOR: On that day, many of the people were baptized, three thousand to be exact. The new believers listened to the teachings of Peter, John and the others. They learned to pray together and to share in the breaking of the bread. Best of all, they received the Holy Spirit, who reminded them that Jesus would be with them forever.

Symbol Dominoes

Pentecost is a good time to learn more about our Christian heritage. Symbols remind us of what we believe as Christians. They prompt us to reflect on the truth behind the symbols. It is important for a full Christian life that students become aware of the meaning of the symbols that are used in the church.

The symbol dominoes game helps students remember what symbols stand for. This is a good follow-up activity after a discussion on symbols. This game can be a learning center activity or it can be played by students who arrive early or finish their work early.

To make a symbol dominoes game, use blank index cards cut in half lengthwise. Nine index cards make eighteen dominoes, enough for a two-player game. Draw a line down the middle of each cut card. Then, on either side of the line put a symbol and its meaning. Each symbol should be used three times. Vary the combination of the symbols on the dominoes. Symbols and their meanings are:

Cross	redemption
Chi Rho	Christ
Dove	Holy Spirit
Butterfly	resurrection
Heart	love
Hand	God
Alpha Omega	eternity
Anchor	hope
Shell	baptism
Book	Bible
Chalice and host	Eucharist
Triangle	Trinity

To play the game, the students place the dominoes face down and mix them up. Each player draws five dominoes. The player selected to go first places any domino face up between the two players. The second player then plays a domino that matches the symbol on either end. If that player does not have a matching domino, he or she draws from the unused pile. The player keeps drawing until a matching domino is found, or until they are all gone. In that case the play passes back to the first player.

Dominoes may be played end to end or at right angles to the ones already played. The only place to add a domino is at either open end. Play continues until one of the players wins by using up all his or her dominoes.

This game is an interesting way to memorize symbols and their meanings. It is fun for the children and can be used again and again.

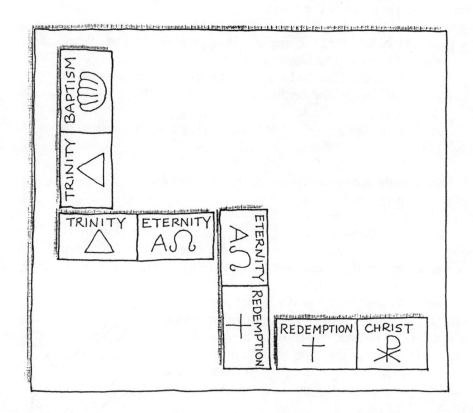

Holy Spirit Prayers

Pentecost is a good time for the students to learn a prayer to the Holy Spirit. The prayer, for example, the "Come, Holy Spirit," can be used at the beginning of class during this season.

Come, Holy Spirit, fill the hearts of your faithful and enkindle in
them the fire of your love.
Send forth your Spirit, and they shall be created; and you will
renew the face of the earth.

Another traditional prayer that is especially good for personal use is this:

Come, Holy Spirit, and direct my every thought,
word and action.

The class members can compose a petition prayer asking the Holy Spirit to work in their lives and in the world. After each petition is read by the teacher, the students respond, "Come, Holy Spirit." This prayer can be changed from week to week to reflect concerns of the class.

We must stress to the students that prayer is essential. Asking for God's help is the first step in a life of Christian witness. We must be people of prayer. We must ask the Holy Spirit to guide us always. May God's will be done in our lives. May we celebrate Pentecost and all the Christian holidays joyfully in his name.

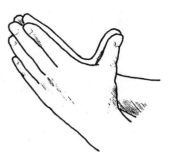

Bibliography of Children's Books

THANKSGIVING

Chandler, Linda S. *When I Talk to God*. Nashville, TN: Broadman Press, 1984. Shows children thanking God for many things in their lives. A good reminder that we need to say thank you to God for our blessings.

Mann, Victor. *He Remembered to Say Thank You*. St. Louis, MO: Concordia Publishing House, 1976. Bible story of one leper who came back to thank Jesus. Excellent story to remind all of us to thank God.

Murphy, Elspeth Campbell. *Everybody Shout Hallelujah*. Elgin, IL: David C. Cook, 1981. About the many gifts God has given us. Helps children learn to praise God.

Odor, Ruth Shannon. *Thank You God for Wonderful Things*. Elgin, IL: The Child's World, 1977. Helps children appreciate the many gifts God has given us in nature. Can lead to a discussion of other things for which we can thank God in our lives.

ADVENT

Collins, David R. *A Spirit of Giving*. Nashville, TN: Broadman Press, 1978. Story of a child who makes a nativity scene for a Christmas contest. Shows children that there are different ways of celebrating Christmas.

Dyer, Heather. *The Good Samaritan*. Elgin, IL: David C. Cook Publishing Co., 1980. Retelling of the bible story of the Good Samaritan. Helps children learn the importance of caring about others.

Frank, Penny. *Jesus Gives the People Food*. Batavia, IL: Lion Publishing Corporation, 1984. Story of the loaves and fishes and how a boy shared what he had. A good reminder to share with others in our lives.

Moncure, Jane Belk. *Caring*. Elgin, IL.: The Child's World, 1980. Presents ways that children can show caring for others. Helps children relate caring about others to people in their own lives.

CHRISTMAS

Galusha, David. *The First Christmas*. Huntington, IN: Our Sunday Visitor, 1981. Tells the story of Jesus' birth in Bethlehem. Helps children visualize the biblical account of Christmas.

Kasuya, Masahiro. *The Way Christmas Came*. Valley Forge, PA: Judson Press, 1973. Recounts the journey of Mary and Joseph to Bethlehem and the visit of the shepherds to the Christ Child. Explains to children the events of the Christmas story.

Moncure, Jane Belk. *The Gift of Christmas*. Elgin, IL: The Child's World, 1979. Simply tells the story of the first Christmas. Helps us remember that Christ is the true gift of Christmas.

Trzeciak, Cathi. *Jesus, the Very Best Christmas Gift of All*. St. Louis, MO: Concordia Publishing House, 1986. Ties the Christmas holiday with the events in Bethlehem long ago. Carries the message that we celebrate Christmas in Jesus' name.

LENT

Dyer, Heather. *The Good Shepherd*. Elgin, IL: David C. Cook Publishing Company, 1980. Retells the biblical story of the shepherd who looks for his lost sheep. Reminds children that Jesus is the Good Shepherd and we are to follow him.

Elmer, Irene. *The Boy Who Ran Away*. St. Louis, MO: Concordia Publishing House, 1964. The story of the prodigal son who was welcomed home by his father. Reminds us of God's forgiveness.

Maier-F., Emil. *Jesus Befriends Zacchaeus*. Nashville, TN: Abingdon Press, 1983. Bible story of Zacchaeus and how he changed his life because of Jesus. Helps us remember to follow the way Jesus taught.

Ulmer, Louise. *Jesus' 12 Disciples*. St. Louis, MO: Concordia Publishing House, 1982. The story of Jesus calling his disciples. It can be used as a discussion starter about how we are all called to a life with him.

EASTER

British and Foreign Bible Society. *Jesus Is Alive*. Minneapolis, MN: Augsburg Publishing House, 1967. The story of Good Friday and Easter. Shows that these events are related and that Jesus did rise from the dead.

Frank, Penny. *The First Easter*. Batavia, IL: Lion Publishing Corporation, 1986. Includes the discovery of the empty tomb and Jesus' appearance to his apostles including Thomas. Helps children recall the Easter events.

Wangerin, Walter, Jr. *The Glory Story*. St. Louis, MO: Concordia Publishing House, 1974. About how one man might have experienced the good news about Jesus' resurrection. Can lead to a discussion of what Easter means.

Wiersum, Beverly Rae. *The Story of Easter for Children*. Milwaukee, WI: Ideals Publishing Company, 1979. Tells the story of the first Easter and shows people going to church on Easter Sunday. Ties together the signs of new life in spring with Easter.

PENTECOST

Frank, Penny. *Good News For Everyone*. Batavia, IL: Lion Publishing Corporation, 1986. Tells the story of Pentecost and how it changed the lives of Jesus'
followers. Can lead to a discussion of how we carry on his work.

Wangerin, Walter, Jr. *O Happy Day!* St. Louis, MO: Concordia Publishing House,
1975. The events of Pentecost are told through the story of a little girl who might
have been there. Can help introduce the biblical account of this day.

Wolcott, Carolyn M. *I Can See What God Does*. Nashville, TN: Abingdon Press,
1969. Helps children discover God's presence through seeing what he does.
Makes the point that when people are kind we can see God's presence.

Wyatt, Mary Moore. *Sharing God's Love With Others*. St. Louis, MO: Concordia
Publishing House, 1979. God's love is described using everyday images. Reminds children that God's love is to be shared.

Notes:

Chapter 1:

1 Patricia L. Mathson, "Prayer Ideas," *Catechist* (July/August 1985), p. 32.

2 Jeanne Coolahan Mueller, *God's People Pray* (Minneapolis, MN: Augsburg Publishing House, 1984), p. 24.

3 Peggy Bradley, *Family Meal Prayers* (Los Angeles, CA: Franciscan Communications), p. 5.

Chapter 3:

1 The Chrismon tree is described by Frances Kipps Spencer, *Chrismons Basic Series* (Danville, VA: Ascension Lutheran Church, 1972), pp. 1-4, 13.

2 Adapted from Joan Lilja, "Jesus Is Born," *Church Teachers* (November/December 1980), p. 91.

3 Adapted from Sue Ruddock, "Church Family Night," *Church Teachers* (November/December 1982), pp. 88-89.

Chapter 4:

1 This idea for a letter to God at the beginning of Lent is from Sister Delores McGinley, "Letters to God," *Religion Teachers Journal* (March 1985), p. 18.

Chapter 5:

1 Patricia L. Mathson, "The Story of Easter," *Church Teachers* (March/April/May 1986), p. 185.

2 Helen Kitchell Evans, "Let Bells Ring," *Rainbows, Dreams, and Butterfly Wings* (March/April 1985), p. 11.

Chapter 6:

1 Gail Moody, "The Story of Pentecost," *Church Teachers* (March/April/May 1985), p. 183.

2 Jeanne Coolahan Mueller, *God's People Pray* (Minneapolis, MN: Augsburg Publishing House, 1984), p. 28.

3 Gwen Costello, "Pentecost Play for Children," *Religion Teachers Journal* (May/June 1979), p. 13.